THY Kingdom Come!

PATRICIA SAID ADAMS

Thy Kingdom Come

Copyright © 2023 by Patricia Said Adams.

PB: ISBN: 978-1-63812-562-4
Ebook ISBN: 978-1-63812-551-8

All rights reserved. No part in this book may be produced and transmitted in any form or by any means, electronic, or mechanical, including photocopying, recording, or by any information storage and retrieval system, without permission in writing from the copyright owner.

The views expressed in this work are solely those of the author and do not necessarily reflect the views of the publisher hereby disclaims any responsibility for them.
Published by Pen Culture Solutions 01/25/2023

Pen Culture Solutions
1-888-727-7204 (USA)
1-800-950-458 (Australia)
support@penculturesolutions.com

DEDICATION

I dedicate this book in loving memory to my late husband, Hank Adams, who always encouraged me in every endeavor, and still seems present in my life.

ACKNOWLEDGMENTS

I offer this book on the kingdom of God back to the Holy Spirit who inspired it in loving service. All error is mine, all inspiration His. As I look back on the four years it took me to write this book in two different versions, I think my ability to express the inspiration is a whole lot better. That being said, the credit really is His. As so often happens when I am writing my weekly blog, I feel that what I am writing gets out ahead of where I actually am. And I am learning what I am writing about it. And so I have to depend a lot on his help.

I want to especially thank Nancy Ashmore of AshmoreINK in Northfield MN for her superb editing skills that took the raw material of what I wrote and turned it into prose that is compelling and still managed to keep my voice throughout.

And I want to remember my children, Jennifer, Jonathan and Peter and their spouses, Jason, Frances and Caroline, and five grandchildren, Jack, Scott, Andrew, Davis and Sarah Grace who are always teaching me how to love. They inspire me with their love and presence in my life.

And finally, thank you, Lord, for being in my life every step of the way even when I was unaware of your presence and love. Everything that I am today, I owe to you loving me, healing me of those things, ideas and assumptions that limited me and calling me always to giving more of myself. Amen.

CONTENTS

Introduction ....p. vii

Part I: Description of the Kingdom .... p. 1

    Chapter 1: The Kingdom is Near ....p. 1
    Chapter 2: The Kingdom is Small, Insignificant,
                Coexists with Evil......................................p. 7
    Chapter 3: The Kingdom is Welcoming, Egalitarian ....p. 13
    Chapter 4: The Kingdom Includes a Judgment Day..............p. 19

Part II: Preparing to Live in the Kingdom .... p. 33

    Chapter 1: Be Born of the water and the Spirit ....p. 35
    Chapter 2: Be Prepared for the Invitation at Any Time..........p. 39
    Chapter 3: Treasure the Kingdom Above All Else ....p. 47
    Chapter 4: Use Your Gifts and Talents,
                Let Them Multiply....................................p. 53
    Chapter 5: Be Empty of Yourself ....p. 59
    Chapter 6: Love Your Neighbor as Yourself ....p. 65
    Chapter 7: Be as a Little Child ....p. 69
    Chapter 8: Love God With All of Yourself.............................p. 73

Part III: Conclusions .... p. 77

About the Author .... p. 87
End Notes .... p. 88
Bibliography.. p. 95

Introduction

Dear Readers: I invite you to read this work about the kingdom of God with an open heart and mind and a willingness to entertain new ideas, to chew on them to see if they have merit and if they will take root in your being. Even if you're able to open up just a little, that might be sufficient to begin to expand the way you think about God and the kingdom and your place in it. These ideas are grounded in Jesus's sayings about the kingdom in the Gospels with the addition of my own experience as a long-time follower of Christ, plus what I have been given to understand in the course of writing this book.

The vision that many Christians hold of the kingdom—that it is heaven, the perfect place where we go after we die if we've been very, very good—limits what we can do and how we can be with God. Subscribing to that view makes us into rule followers seeking to be perfect in obeying every command. Basing our actions on a literal reading of Jesus's command to "be perfect, therefore, as your heavenly father is perfect,"[1] we restrict our behavior and our thinking in our relationship with God to just one facet of who we can be in loving God. To dig a little deeper into the meaning of this phrase, look at the meaning of the ancient Greek word, teleios. It is translated as "perfect" in our modern Bibles. But in ancient Greek the meaning was more about perfection in the sense of being complete or whole.[2] So we might reword the passage to read like this: be whole and complete as your father in heaven is whole and complete.

Not only does trying to be perfect limit who we are and how we can be with God, but it also limits how we think about God. God then becomes the rule enforcer who asks for more and more perfect behavior from us and punishes us for any infractions. God is limited to being the big, capricious Parent in the Sky throwing thunderbolts at us from his chariot.

I am not at all sure that we can begin to wrap our minds around God in his totality—Creator of an incredibly diverse and interdependent universe, Sustainer of all life, Being without beginning or end, Love itself, the One who wants an intimate relationship with each one of us and on and on. Then there is the Trinity, how God appears in three guises or persons, how he still creates in this world, how he relates to his creatures, how he holds together the creation, how he loves and sustains. I can't even begin to imagine the Mind that created the Earth and its living things. Can you?

Instead, let's look to the many references in Jesus' teachings to God as the One who embraces and loves and forgives us, who wants to partner with us in realizing the person each of us was created to be. The "flowers of the field"[3] and the Parable of the Lost or Prodigal Son[4] are just two that come to mind. God takes care of all our needs; Jesus asks, "why are we anxious, then?" And in the Parable of Prodigal Son God welcomes back his errant sons and daughters, no matter what they have done with their inheritance. Don't these two passages just puncture that idea of the Punishing Parent?

Thinking rigidly about our relationship with God severely limits who we are with God. It keeps us more on the human side of the equation than on the kingdom side. It keeps us as children rather than collaborators or co-creators with God. And it certainly doesn't invite the life-transforming action of the Holy Spirit to change us into human beings who can love, who can live in this world and yet not be of this world.

THY KINGDOM COME!

* * * * *

After his baptism and the time in the wilderness recounted in the Gospel of Luke Jesus went up to the synagogue in Nazareth where he unrolled the scroll to this saying from Isaiah:

The Spirit of the Lord is on me,

because he has anointed me

to proclaim good news to the poor.

He has sent me to proclaim freedom

   for the prisoners

     and recovery of sight for the blind.

To set the oppressed free,

To proclaim the year of the Lord's favor.[5]

Here Jesus proclaims his purpose and launches his ministry to spread this good news—the gospel about the kingdom of God—to all who came to hear him and to witness his healings.

The kingdom is a major theme of the Synoptic Gospels; there are myriads of references to it in the teachings and in the parables. "The kingdom of God or Heaven is like…" is a common introduction to the topic. Even when he doesn't explicitly introduce the kingdom, as in the Sermon on the Mount, it is still the topic at hand. He came to proclaim good news to the poor, freedom for the prisoner, sight for the blind, to set the captive free, to proclaim the year of the Lord's favor! Jesus is quoting from Isaiah 61:1-3:

"1The Spirit of the Lord GOD is upon me, Because the LORD has anointed me To bring good news to the afflicted; He has sent me to bind up the brokenhearted, To proclaim liberty to captives And freedom to prisoners; 2To proclaim the favorable year of the LORD And the day of vengeance of our God; To comfort all who mourn, 3To grant those who mourn in Zion, Giving them a garland instead of ashes, The oil of gladness instead of mourning, The mantle of praise instead of a spirit of fainting. So they will be called oaks of righteousness, The planting of the LORD, that He may be glorified...."

The favorable year of the Lord—when Israelites who were enslaved were to be set free—might be called the joy of the kingdom now come on earth, proclaimed by Jesus Christ. For how could it not be experienced as joy for the blind to see? For the captive to be his own person again? For the poor to be celebrated and freed, and for the prisoner to get out of jail? He is proclaiming that in God's favor, in God's kingdom, there are all these freedoms to be enjoyed, to bring joy into one's life. Even the day of vengeance seems to fit here: all justice will be restored, Mercy and love will be the currency of the kingdom, to the joy of all.

God has sent his prophets and his son to proclaim his kingdom again and again in the Scriptures. For we, being fickle and inconstant human beings, need to be reminded again and again, that we could live in God's favor in his kingdom. All our needs would be met. We would be transformed into people who could love like God loves. We would live out our purpose here on earth.

In Part I we'll be looking at how Jesus described the kingdom of God. Then in Part II we'll tackle the teachings about how we can prepare to live in the kingdom. And in Part III we'll discuss the implications for you and me in his descriptions and teachings. I suggest that you bookmark the beginning of the footnotes at the end of the book. That way you can easily find the Biblical and other references cited.

PART I: DESCRIPTION OF THE KINGDOM

CHAPTER 1

The Kingdom is Near

Every time we pray the Lord's Prayer, we say "thy kingdom come." Do we even know what we are saying when we repeat these familiar words? Jesus was certain about the kingdom; he taught about it throughout his ministry. But does the interpretation we've inherited, that the kingdom is only in the afterlife, in heaven, make sense in light of his teachings?

In the three Synoptic Gospels Jesus spoke of the kingdom in the present tense: the kingdom is "at hand,"[6] "has come near,"[7] is "within you,"[8] is "in your midst,"[9] and is "already among you."[10] All these suggest that the kingdom is not to come, but is present now, within us as well as among us.

If we believe what Jesus said, then why don't we experience the kingdom? Why don't we see it before our eyes?

Jesus seems to be saying that the kingdom is not so evident, not obvious, but that it is still here, waiting to be discovered. And that it is everywhere. "Among us" implies a community. "Within us" implies that we can access it within ourselves. "In your midst"—again it is here, maybe right alongside of us, inside and outside of us. Ubiquitous, ever-present, everywhere, an inner and outer experience. A potential that needs to be realized. And yet we do not see it. To do that we have to not only open our eyes but we also have to look for it. One of the richest places to do that is in the parables of Jesus, the stories he told to instruct those who would follow him.

The Parable of the Leaven

The Parable of the Leaven continues to expound upon the theme that the kingdom is everywhere, though it is not always visible to us: "The kingdom of heaven is like yeast that a woman took and mixed into about sixty pounds of flour until it worked all through the dough."[11] Jesus is making the point here that the yeast is everywhere in the bread, yet not distinguishable from it.[12] It works its way silently but is a key ingredient in making the bread rise and be edible.

Similarly the kingdom is hidden from us, protected from sight, yet significant in our lives. It is found in the structures that support life, in the intricacies of creation, in the shifting of weather patterns and in the more rigid structures of DNA, in the interconnectedness and interdependence of all life, in the beauty of nature, in every given thing and in all the things we take for granted.

While we see what is manifest in the world, the kingdom is not obvious until we seek to know all the motivating principles in our world, to know what causes the effects. Clearly, many of the causes of what is happening in the world are human, even evil. There is another option for us, though, if we will seek it out. Hints of God's action, God's kingdom in our world, are found in the Bible and in our lives, like the flavor or aroma of yeast sometimes obvious in the risen and baked bread. But we must pay them heed. We might write them off as coincidences, but we see them in spontaneous healings that doctors cannot justify. We see them in serendipity, happy coincidences in things just happening to go right for us. We experience them when someone loves us as we are. We see them when we gaze in awe at a sunset, when we experience the presence of God as we open ourselves to him. These are traces, small tastes of the leaven of the kingdom in the real world. If we would open our eyes, we would notice so much more.[13]

Jesus, at the end of his days on Earth, repeatedly assured his followers that he was going ahead to hold a place for them with his Father and leaving the Holy Spirit to be with them and much more.[14] On the day of Pentecost his disciples, inspirited by the Holy Spirit, took up Jesus's mission in spreading the good news of the kingdom.

And so we are similarly encouraged throughout the Gospels[15] to follow Jesus and his teachings, embracing the kind of relationship he had with his "Abba" in order that we, too, can be empowered to in our own way bring in the kingdom on this earth.[16] (I believe that this is our unique purpose, implied in our creation.) Implanted in us, if we turn toward God and away from our very human ways, is the Spirit of God that would heal and teach and lead us to our own divine purpose.

Jesus's contemporaries were expecting a Messiah, an earthly king like King David who would rule over them, defeating the Roman Empire and establishing a physical kingdom in which they could thrive. Jesus says to Pilate at his trial, however, that "my kingdom is not of this world."[17] The kingdom of God is here, there, and everywhere, he is telling us, but it does not follow the rules of an earthly kingdom; God is not going to send his armies to fight off this threat, to drive off the Romans. It is God's kingdom that Jesus represents, not a place as much as a state of mind that is present everywhere, at least potentially, something that everyone could participate in if s/he will meet certain conditions. (We'll address those conditions in Part III.)

I am impelled to ask: If the kingdom is near and it's everywhere and yet not visible, then what is the key to entry? There must be an entry point, must be a way for us to access it. Clearly Jesus is one key. Indeed, many Christians believe that Jesus is the only way. And yet the kingdom is potentially available to all. That means there has to be a key within each of us, Christian or not, a way for all of us to access it.

Here is where the soul comes in. Whether it is God within us or the place wherein God can communicate with us remains a mystery to me, but the soul lies deep in the unconscious. It has two functions: 1) to contain and to advance the agenda set for each of us at our conception/creation and 2) to be the means by which the Holy Spirit can communicate with us. It accomplishes these by providing a way for us to hear that "still, small voice" within of God and promoting our unique calling within us. It calls us throughout our lifetime to our true purpose; it never ceases to try to draw us toward God. It's up to the individual whether s/he ever pays attention to the soul, but the soul doesn't stop trying to connect with the person.

The kingdom is so incorporated into the fabric of creation that it is easily overlooked when a person is in the grip of the cultural paradigm. It can be experienced, though, and even sought after, if one is aware of its existence. Whether we choose to acknowledge the kingdom or not, it is here, there, and everywhere. It exists out in the world, it is discoverable; the same is true within us. It is not a physical place, but a state of mind that lies dormant in us, ready to grow and flourish if we pay attention to it and embrace it.

From the unseen, but very present nature of the kingdom described above, we will turn in the next chapter to its seeming insignificant size.

CHAPTER 2

The Kingdom is Small, Insignificant, Co-exists with Evil

Let's continue our investigation of the nature of the kingdom by looking at parables based in nature itself.

The Parables of the Mustard Seed and the Seed and the Sower

The kingdom was compared by Jesus to a mustard seed,[18] a tiny seed, insignificant almost, that can grow into a 12-foot-high bush or small tree. How are they similar?

The kingdom can be overlooked easily and yet its seed has enormous potential.

When ground, the mustard seed produces a pretty zesty accompaniment to food, so it is full of life.

The mustard seed grows to be so huge that it can accommodate the birds of the air.

The kingdom is hidden, tiny, insignificant—until it takes root in us. And then—wow!—we experience a complete change in attitude, a change grown out of the seed of a different way of living.

The potential in the seed, and in the kingdom, is not at all commensurate with its size. Surprising. It will house the birds, representative of the Spirit, giving all the birds need for life and shade and home. Birds—air, breath, spirit.

Jesus's reference to the birds of the air suggests another thing about the kingdom and its inhabitants—they do just what they were designed to do,[19] and God takes care of their needs. Is Jesus perhaps suggesting that the mustard plant can house the Spirit of God, too?

One doesn't need to see a bird up close in order to identify individual species of birds. They can be recognized by their profiles or by the way they fly. Take, for instance, the cardinal and the chickadee. The cardinal zeroes in on his target, be it a feeder or a bush. I have seen a cardinal feed its mate. A chickadee, on the other hand, swoops in arcs toward its desires, and I've rarely seen a pair of chickadees at my feeder.

These two species model what we are also to become—a person who is and does what he or she was designed to do, after we have thrown off everything—every thought, action, assumption, and expectation—that isn't totally natural to us. After we have stripped down to the essence of who we were created to be, letting go of the cultural conditioning and the familial training that goes against everything that God would have us be.

The "sower of seed" is a common theme in parables about the kingdom. God is sowing seed everywhere[20]—on rocky soil where it might sprout quickly and then die for lack of nutrients, among the thorns where it is difficult to take root, on good soil where it sprouts and thrives. The kingdom flourishes where the conditions are right for its growth. The seeds represent God's invitations that he strews everywhere in hopes that people will accept his offer to come into relationship with him.

I have this picture in my mind of God eternally sowing endless quantities of seed—think blessings and grace and his word—and having most of it fall on hard, thorny, or hostile soil. And yet he keeps sowing the seed, knowing that occasionally it will fall on soil that will actively promote its growth. It's astonishing to me how God scatters his invitations for us and waits for us to accept them. He doesn't bang us over the head or wrestle us to the ground to force us to accept them. (He obviously is not a human being or he would have given up on us long ago!)

The Parable of the Wheat and Tares, the Parable of the Net

In the Parable of the Wheat and Tares,[21] the servants are told not to pull the weeds that are growing up with the wheat so that they don't inadvertently pull up some of the wheat, too. (My NIV Study Bible suggests that the weeds are likely to be darnel,[22] which greatly resembles wheat early in its growing process but is easily distinguished from wheat at harvest time.) The Parable of the Net[23] speaks of the harvesting of fish. In the catch are good fish and rotten fish, but, again, we are enjoined not to try to sort them before the harvest. (I think their smell might make them easily distinguishable at that point!)

In both these parables the plants and weeds and the good and the bad fish are too similar to separate before the harvest, but at harvest time sorting them out is no problem. These stories of Jesus echo his teaching: "By their fruit you will know them... A good tree cannot bear bad fruit and a bad tree cannot bear good fruit."[24]

One thing Jesus seems to suggest in these parables is that there is no problem with the good and the evil growing up together or in being in the world together. We will tackle the Judgment Day parables in Chapter 4 of Part II, but here apparently the evil takes nothing away from the good nor does it dilute the good or affect its existence. Having the good defines the evil, of course, and vice versa. For how would we recognize evil if the good were not standing right beside it? And how would we choose good if we couldn't see the contrast?

One of the great challenges to me in loving God has been to accept that God is not going to wipe out evil, period. (I don't think that God created evil, but in giving us free will he created the possibility of evil.) God has had many opportunities to eliminate evil since the times of Noah and the flood, but he has kept his covenant with Noah.[25] He is not going to make it easy for me or for you to choose good. We're going to have to struggle with our own part human/part divine nature until we clearly are on the side of good in our lives. Darn!

The Parable of the Growing Seed

In the Parable of the Growing Seed, which appears only in Mark,[26] Jesus suggests that the process by which the seed sprouts and thrives is mysterious. The sower can provide good soil and water and still the growth takes place in the dark; we don't know why, in the same perfect conditions, one seed spouts and another languishes. The same is true with the kingdom: Two seemingly dedicated people can have widely varying success with having the kingdom become a growing reality within them.

Think a bit about what a seed is. It is a potential plant or, as an ovum, a potential animal or human. Everything that this plant or animal or human is to do and be is contained in the seed's few cells—its genus, its species, the specific nourishment it will need in its first stages of growth.

THY KINGDOM COME!

In the case of human beings, the DNA in the ovum/sperm combo contains everything that someone today has—everything, that is, except the conditioning/nurture we receive. The "soil"—read "family" and "culture"—in which a human grows up does not change the basic design of his/her creation, but, depending upon how benign or toxic conditions are, environment can change the whole trajectory of a life.

The goal of persons seeking the kingdom as the place in which to dwell is—with God's help—to strip themselves of the thoughts and desires implanted since birth that would derail their most natural development and life. For in order to enter the kingdom one must go through the narrow gate[27] in as natural a state, as close to the created self, as one can be—divested of all the conditioning that interferes with our giving of our most natural self, so that, like the flowers of the field and the birds of the air,[28] we are doing what we were designed to do.

And what is this conditioning that keeps us out of the kingdom? The assumptions and preconceptions and expectations that have been conditioned in us from our birth that keep us in the "real" world, tied to its goals for us, rather than putting the kingdom of God first among all things. We'll address this more in Part II. For now I would like to point out that these things that we espouse that are foreign to us have a number of sources: our family of origin, any group we have belonged to, the culture in which we were raised, the church in which we grew up and to which we may still belong. All these foster a view of life that is limited and often self-serving. They often promote a view of God that is not based in reality and a view of ourselves that is similarly flawed.

Self-esteem is not the problem, at least not self-esteem as it is viewed in our culture today. The problem is that we don't see reality with clear lenses; we don't see the way God created us to see. All our experiences, particularly the training of our childhoods, color how we see ourselves and the world.

We live, for instance, in a culture that promotes punishment as a way of training children. And it's in the punishments that a child receives that he comes to misunderstand how long it takes to train anyone and that every failure becomes a blot on his inner notion of self. Eventually he becomes an adult who is more comfortable with punishment than with a real assessment, who adopts as his self-image a flawed view that keeps him tied to the culture which has trained him in ways unnatural to his true self.

When it comes to God and the kingdom, we often view them through this childhood/cultural lens and perceive God as the same kind of parent that we had as a child but bigger and wiser. Can we truly see the kingdom through these flawed lenses? Can we see ourselves as we really are? It is no wonder that the kingdom is hidden from us and that it takes a real turnaround, a repentance of the way we have viewed things, to begin to embrace a clear view of reality and of ourselves. It is then, as we begin to let the idea of kingdom of God take hold in us, that we begin to see ourselves and life as they truly are.

In Chapter Three we will look at the welcoming and egalitarian aspects of the kingdom.

CHAPTER 3

The Kingdom is Welcoming and Egalitarian

The Parable of the Prodigal Son

Turning next to the Parable of the Prodigal [Lost] Son in the Gospel of Luke,[29] we see the father take great pleasure in the arrival of the son who was lost. Once given to profligate living, the younger son now comes home, repentant. He has decided that he would prefer to work as a servant for his father than as a slave for others—this is the state he has been reduced to.

The father has kept an eye out for the son in case he should return. He takes great joy in his son's return, no matter what he has done. More important than his prior behavior is the fact that his son has turned back to his father (to the kingdom). The younger son, who is steeped in shame and guilt, probably expects punishment, but he finds no such thing—all he is offered is welcome and celebration.

When the father welcomes the younger son with a feast and restores to him his inheritance, the older son who has been there all along sulks. He has been dutiful, carefully doing everything expected of him. He has totally missed out on the benefits of the kingdom, however: He has not felt the love of his father (even though it is evident to everyone else), and he is filled with resentment about his brother. He is the Pharisee keeping to the letter of the law and missing the spirit of it, which is love.

In very real but different ways, neither of the sons have been in the kingdom. When the older one complains about the celebration, his father tells him, "My son, you are always with me, and everything I have is yours. But we had to celebrate and be glad, because this brother of yours was dead and is alive again; he was lost and is found."[30]

The important thing in the kingdom is that we show up, no matter when, no matter what we have done. We will be welcomed when we have turned back, when we have "repented," to God, when we let go of all that has kept us out of the kingdom, whether it is poor choices or misunderstandings of what the kingdom is about. The blessings we receive are the same, whether we have been there all along or have just recently arrived.

The dutiful son resents the celebration the father offers to the wayward son. But the prodigal's return does not threaten his true inheritance. The inheritance is the same for everyone who enters the kingdom. It is a real home in the arms of God. It is a participation in the bounty of the universe. It is the free-flowing love which streams steadily out of God and into everyone (whether they are aware of it or not) and out again to everyone else. It is being gifted with the fruit of the Spirit—peace, love, joy, patience, kindness, goodness, self-control, and faithfulness—all gradually assimilated into the life of each person who has the deep relationship with God.[31] It is the very real freedom to be who we were created to be—free of pretense, free of other people's goals—the freedom to take up our lives as we were intended to live and to be.

So much in embracing the kingdom and putting it first in our lives depends on our ability to take in God's love for us. Both brothers in the Parable of the Prodigal Son are not treating themselves or others well—one squandering an inheritance, the other seemingly accepting the kingdom, but resenting another person who seeks it. My experience is that there is a law of human behavior operating here: that we can only love others to the extent that we love ourselves. Jesus suggests this in the two Great Commandments. First we are to love God with all of ourselves. Secondly, we are to love our neighbor as we love ourselves. We cannot give love when we've never felt loved. How can we put God and the kingdom first if we have not begun to fill the hole that is deep inside of us? We are still the needy one, not the one who can give.

The prodigal son has taken the first step toward loving himself—he's come home to his father, his true home. The other son has yet to take the first step. He cannot even welcome his brother, because he himself does not feel his father's love and embrace. Until he takes the first step towards loving himself, which for him, I think, might be to ask his father to forgive him his hypocritical ways, he will not be in the kingdom. It isn't his home; he doesn't feel loved; he can't love others.

The Parable of the Workers in the Vineyard

Jesus goes into great detail in the Parable of the Workers in the Vineyard about the landowner who contracted with various workers at different hours of the day to work in his vineyard.[32] At the end of the day all the workers were paid the same wages whether they started in the early morning hours or were hired late in the day. The workers who started early grumbled about the pay for the latecomers, but the landowner reminded them that they had agreed to work for a denarius and that was what he paid them and everyone else. Grudgingly they admitted that he was right.

The landowner continues, saying that he has a right to do with his money what he wants: "Or are you envious because I am generous? So the last will be first and the first last."[33]

The money in this tale represents the generosity of God toward us. He rewards us for our labor on his behalf, but all of us will get the same blessings whether we are new to the kingdom or have been his servant for our whole lives. The equal treatment by the landowner is startling to us, because it is unknown in the material world. But the kingdom is not about status or time spent there or any other human measure.

Both of these parables, the Prodigal Son and the Workers in the Vineyard, remind us that the blessings in the kingdom fall to everyone equally. There is no advantage in being an early arrival, there is no advantage in being the older and more dutiful son, no disadvantage in having made bad choices in your life. Everyone in the kingdom is equal. I should say, too, that there is no advantage in being white or black or Asian or Native. None in being a male or female. Slave or free.[34] All are welcome in the kingdom and benefit in the same ways.

The Parable of the Unmerciful Servant

Let's look at the Parable of the Unmerciful Servant[35] to see another aspect of the kingdom. At his servant's urging for patience and his promise to pay what was owed, a master took pity on the servant who owed him 10,000 bags of gold and canceled the debt. The same servant, his debt now forgiven, then found another servant who owed him 100 silver coins; he choked him and demanded that he pay back what he owed. The second servant asked for his patience and swore he would pay him back. The first servant refused and had the man thrown into prison until he could repay him. His fellow servants, outraged at his treatment, told their master what had happened.

The master called in the first servant and berated him: "You begged for patience and I showed you mercy and cancelled your debt. Shouldn't you have done the same for your fellow servant?" He then turned him over to the jailers to be tortured until he paid back what he owed.

This parable hardly needs interpretation: We are to give to others what we have been given—mercy, love, forgiveness, patience. We don't hear too much about the Golden Rule any more, but it is a good standard of behavior for us: "Do to others as you would have them do to you."[36]

Obviously there was a social or economic status difference between the servant who owed 10,000 bags of gold and the one who owed 100 silver coins.[37] The first one must have been quite wealthy on his own to have borrowed so much. The second one probably owed a day's wages,[38] no small matter for a day laborer to pay back. And yet the loans must have been freely given in the first place. That's the other message in this parable. What we have is freely given, but it is on loan to us during our lifetime. It belongs to God, not to us, and "it is beyond our capacity to repay."[39] Forgiveness and generosity, mercy and love—what we have been given—are to be shared, not hoarded.

There is a further implication in this parable: that our forgiveness is tied to our forgiving others. We are to give freely what we have been given.

The three parables—the Prodigal Son, the Workers in the Vineyard, and the Unmerciful Servant—offer glimpses of the kingdom that are radically different from the way human cultures usually operate. Even today, the behavior they lay bare is startling to us.

To get past the seeming unfairness within these tales, we have to think deeply about the kingdom. When we do that, we see that they show a God who gives all he promises to us and more. The kingdom is a place where everyone is welcome, no matter what. Everyone is equal, period. And everyone is expected to pass on what they have received.

In Chapter 4 we'll look at the passages, particularly in Matthew, about the judgment day.

CHAPTER 4

The Kingdom Includes a Judgment Day

In this last set of parables, the focus is on the apocalyptic nature of the kingdom, the kingdom of God that will come with the Second Coming of Christ who will judge everyone, embracing the good who will have eternal life and discarding the bad. Most of the apocalyptic teachings come from Matthew's gospel. He reports six times that there will be weeping and gnashing of teeth;[40] Luke mentions this only once,[41] and Mark and John not at all. In this chapter we'll be looking at Matthew's interpretation of this day of judgment, which has influenced so much of Christian thought about the apocalypse.[42] My thesis is that he is describing a personal judgment day and not a global one, that when Christ resides in us any evil tendencies cannot stay.

After Jesus's death and ascension, his followers expected him to return at any time to bring in this day of judgment. By 324 AD the belief in the Second Coming was incorporated officially in the Nicene Creed.[43] Since then many Christian sects and leaders (including Rev. Jerry Falwell, as recently as 1999) have been convinced that they knew the date of Judgment Day.[44]

This is a curious thing for those of us who don't believe in magical, mystical possibilities. How do we approach this subject?

As post-modern deconstructionists, we tend to be very suspicious of anything that can't be scientifically proven: miracles, the apocalypse, etc., are all suspect. The writer of Matthew had no such hesitations. His Gospel is filled with miracles, healings, and talk of the end times and the gnashing of teeth that will occur when the sheep are separated from the goats.

I tackle this idea of judgment and separating the sheep from the goats with some trepidation. Frankly, I don't like the idea of a hellfire-and-damnation God. I was raised in a church with such beliefs and would prefer to ignore these passages altogether. I have learned of the utility of bringing fresh eyes to difficult passages to see what wisdom they offer, however, and Matthew definitely contains keys to understanding the standards of the kingdom that we are addressing in this book. In other words, these passages are *not to be omitted*.

The Parable of the Net and the Parable of the Weeds

"Come, follow me and I will send you out to fish for people,"[45] says Jesus in Matthew Chapter 4, calling to the men he is inviting to become his disciples, the men who will help him "catch" those who will follow him. There is more about fishing in the Parable of the Net in Matthew Chapter 13[46]: After a net is let down into the sea, a harvest of fish is taken to shore to be separated, with the good fish being put into baskets to sell or take home and the bad fish being thrown away.

In this and in the Parable of the Weeds[47] which precedes it in the same chapter, bad fish and good, weeds and wheat, exist together in their environment until the harvest, at which time the bad fish and the weeds are identified and thrown out.

It is no mystery why these examples, especially of fishing, were put forward in Matthew. Since the beginning of Chapter 11, Jesus had been preaching in the towns of Galilee. Fisherman plied their trade all around the lake. They and their families would have readily understood the images and symbols in the Parable of the Net.

We need further explanation today, however. Sure, some fish were more preferable as food than others, but what are "bad" ones? Jesus doesn't say what makes a fish bad, but Matthew uses the Greek word *sapros*, an adjective that means "bad, rotten, decayed, unwholesome."[48]

Contemplating these two parables plunges us into the mystery of how good and evil coexist and why. Why doesn't God just take care of the evil so we don't have to deal with it?

We each have within us impulses toward good and toward evil. We determine how we live our lives. God as Creator determines the rules and sets the consequences for disobeying them any way he wants. In Matthew, though, Jesus doesn't just suggest consequences: He calls for a Judgment Day with a fiery furnace to burn off the dross: the sinful and the evil. As he explains to his disciples in the Parable of the Weeds,[49] the Son of Man is the sower, the field the world, the good seeds those who live in the kingdom, the enemy is the devil, the weeds the devil's own. At judgment time the Son of Man will send his "angels and they will weed out of his kingdom everything that causes sin and all who do evil. They will throw them into the fiery furnace, where there will be weeping and gnashing of teeth."[50]

But ... don't we face God's judgment every day within ourselves? Don't we feel guilty for words said that we wish we could take back? For mistreating someone? For not being true to our own values? Don't we die a bit for everything we do that we're not proud of?

Is Jesus calling for a Judgment Day or is he perhaps describing what happens inside us when we fall short of the mark? We certainly judge ourselves when we miss that mark, but in accumulating "bad marks" against our own selves—not from God's judgment, but from our own—don't we also lose our ability to enjoy, to love, to truly give?

There is another implication in these two parables, which is that the Judgment Day is also a personal one: When Jesus comes into our lives, he separates out the evil tendencies and casts them out of us. As we face what we have been, there will be a wrenching time and then a letting go of the "sin" since it cannot exist in Christ's presence. It has to fall away.

Is Jesus teaching what we already know to be true? Which is that we are not full of life, not the wheat that is ready to harvest. That we have fallen short again of what we were created to do, living lives dependent on and defined by the culture and not as we were created to be by God.

We hope to get a pass from God for that, but I don't think we are forgiven for leading someone else's life until we stop trying to be someone else. If we are true to God's expectations of us and of our own true selves (which I believe are the same thing), then we needn't live in fear of Judgment Day. In living as we were created to be we are choosing to live on God's side, in the kingdom.

We have an interior calibrator, our conscience, for distinguishing truth from lies, love from hate, and faith from fear. Each time we ignore the red flags our conscience sends up to warn us that we are violating our own standards, we die a little. Each time we cross the line we invite the exacting judgment of the Lord. We don't have to wait for the eternal judgment; we are judged by what we do and fail to do even as we do it.

Like heaven, judgment is not a distant reality, due at the Second Coming of Christ; we live with it every day. What Christ does when we invite him in is to transform all those tendencies toward egotism and even evil into an ability to love and serve. To speak in threshing terms, the grain is the good in us. It grows from the good seed; it needs to be separated out from the waste products of the process—the husks or chaff and the stalks and any weeds that were harvested as well. God only wants to save the product, the fruit, of the harvest, in this case the grain. All else is blown away. Then we are fully alive and living in the kingdom.

In these very short parables and Jesus's explanation of them we find an explanation for the question I raised earlier about why God does not just zap away the evil. Jesus is implying that the good needs to be nurtured alongside the evil of the world, that evil loses out in the end, and does not pollute the good even while growing up around it.

Is there a further implication that the good needs the evil in some way right beside it in order to come into fruition? Is the good strengthened by the contact with evil? Seemingly. This is part of the mystery of the kingdom of heaven, a paradox that **our minds really have to wrestle with to understand.**

The Parable of the Sheep and the Goats

At the end of Chapter 3, I wrote, "The kingdom is a place where everyone is welcome, no matter what. Everyone is equal, period. And everyone is expected to pass on what they have received." Everyone is welcome in the kingdom, but there is one condition for entry in the kingdom: to put the kingdom of God, the love of God before anything else.[51] This is not to be just a belief, but a commitment to live the first of the Two Great

Commandments: to love God with all your heart, soul, mind and strength.[52]

In his Parable of the Sheep and the Goats,[53] Jesus defines who is welcome in the kingdom and who is not. The difference between the sheep who helped others, serving Jesus in another person, and the goats, who refused to help another in need, is huge. Though sheep and goats provide much of the same products for their owners—milk, wool, cheese, offspring—the sheep are followers and the goats are not.[54]

That's the rule in the kingdom; followers of God are welcome. The sheep, those who will stay with him in the kingdom, he gathers at his right hand, because they have fed him, given him drink, invited him when a stranger, clothed him, cared for him when he was sick and visited him in prison any time they took care of another in need whom Jesus called the least of his brothers.[55] In this passage Jesus repeats this list four times, twice to the sheep as he praises their actions[56] and twice to the goats as he points out their refusal to help, giving emphasis to the criteria.[57]

This imagery of the separation of the sheep and the goats has captured the imagination of people from the first century to now. Artists like Michelangelo have painted it. Books like Dante's Inferno have been written about it. Movies like *The Apocalypse* (2007) have been released about this topic. We've been waiting for 2,000-plus years for the Second Coming of Christ. Throughout those two millennia, end times groups have been predicting when it would be—so far without success.

Is it possible that we were all wrong? That Jesus meant something personal and immediate rather than a global phenomenon? That he was describing in the gnashing of teeth and the wailing what happens *within* the individual when Christ is invited to take up residence there? And that the

Second Coming is the coming of the legions following Christ, being love in this world, being his hands and feet, creating a real community of people where everyone is welcome and equal? Not just Jesus sitting on the judgment throne all by himself?

Goats carve out their own paths, unlike sheep, who are followers. When Christ resides within us, there is no room for "goats"—no room for those stubborn places where we are inflexible, unwilling, or unable to change and wanting our own way in life; for attachments to the past, the culture, and our own creature comforts; for unhealed traumas, unhealthy thoughts, and fierce independence.

Sheep, unlike goats, which are horned, have no natural defense system other than huddling together in flocks, which provides more safety than being alone. They represent the vulnerable, more childlike dependence, the willingness to follow and to be led. They also represent the community of faith.

When Christ gets hold of us, dwells in us, when we have surrendered our lives to him, the goats are ousted. The sheep get more space; they fall into line faster, are more desirous of a leader and direction than any goat ever was.

The Parable of the Wedding Banquet

In the Parable of the Wedding Banquet, in which none of the original invitees to the banquet came to the event, the king sends out his servants to the street corners to bring all who could come, "the bad as well as the good," as the texts put it.[58] The king took exception to one of the "guests," however—someone who was not dressed in clothes fit for the feast. Apparently he was not ready to enter, had not made the proper preparations.

Likewise, throughout Matthew's Gospel there are indications that those who dwell in the kingdom also dwell in the whole population, which includes the hostile, the invitees who refused to show up, and the people on the streets—including the man who represents all who have not dressed for, are not ready for, the banquet.

In the Beatitudes Jesus talks of the kingdom of heaven belonging to two groups: the poor in spirit[59] and those who are persecuted because of their righteousness.[60] To be "poor in spirit" is to recognize how much we need God in our lives, to fulfill who we were created to be, to fill us up with love, to show us the way to rich, abundant life, to bring us out of our preoccupation with ourselves so that we can truly love him and others. Notice that here Jesus says the kingdom "belongs" to them. He uses the present tense. The kingdom is not some future reward, but a reality right now.

The kingdom also belongs to those who are persecuted because they are righteous.[61] They follow the laws *and* they love God and their neighbor. There is little approbation for them either in 1st-century Palestine or 21st-century America. They model behavior that is difficult for most people to follow, so we try to tear them down rather than allow ourselves to be confronted by what they model. Many have been martyred for Christ's sake over the Christian centuries; even today some are persecuted for their beliefs. It is a dangerous thing to hold up a cold mirror reflecting behavior to people who have no intention of following the law or commandments.

Those who practice and teach the commandments also belong in the kingdom of heaven,[62] as do any whose righteousness surpasses that of the Pharisees.[63] (Jesus had special contempt for those who were steeped in the law, but who followed it so faithfully—to the letter—that they forgot the purpose of the law, the spirit of the law.) Those who seek his kingdom[64] first above all else and those who do the will of his Father[65] dwell in the kingdom, as do those who have knowledge of the secrets of the kingdom.[66]

Speaking from Capernaum,[67] Jesus also spoke of many coming from the east and west to join the feast with Abraham, Isaac, and Jacob in the kingdom. Those who are like little children[68] or humbled like a child[69] also belong in the kingdom.

Look at what we have so far: the "poor in spirit," those persecuted for righteousness, those who practice and teach the commandments, those whose righteousness surpasses that of the Pharisees, those who seek first his kingdom, those who do the will of the Father, those from beyond Galilee, and those who are children before the Lord, humble, looking to God as parent. What Jesus is describing are ones who have a child-like relationship with the Father, who follow his commandments, who put God first. These are the ones who belong in the kingdom of heaven.[70]

But there are more. In the Parable of the Wise and Foolish Virgins, Jesus welcomes those who are ready with oil for their lamps.[71] He calls out those who multiplied what was entrusted to them in the Parable of the Talents or Bags of Gold[72] and in the Parable of the Workers[73] in the Vineyard he raises up those who are "last": the workers who started work in the late afternoon and were paid the same wage as those who began in the morning.

The "sheep" are those who are ready to enter the kingdom through their relationship with God, who put God and his kingdom first, who suffer for his sake, who are like little children to God, those who are willing to do his will and who are willing to follow where he leads.

God clearly has his standards for who will enter the kingdom. It is also easy to misinterpret those standards. The task for us is not following the rules, taking care of others, and not doing evil. You can be a "good person" and not enter the kingdom. The true tests to me are the answers to these questions:

Do we have a deep relationship with God? Is God and his kingdom first in our hearts and minds?

Can we do all the above as a child who trusts and loves his Divine Parent so much that she or he will do what the parent asks, just because he or she knows that the parent loves him and has his best interests at heart?

Will we take Christ's offered hand and let him lead us where he will with total trust and love?

Are we "poor in spirit" enough to let him fill us with all he has in store for us?

If we can answer "yes!" to these questions, then we are preparing to enter the kingdom.

Let's turn to the "goats," those who are definitely not preparing for life in the kingdom. Among them are the wicked,[74] the enemy [of the kingdom],[75] those who show no mercy even when they have been treated mercifully,[76] hypocrites,[77] those who are weeds among the wheat,[78] those who break the commands and teach others to do the same,[79] and whoever causes sin and does evil.[80]

Also included with the "goats" are those who have refused to help others. These "goats" will never enter the kingdom of heaven because they do not or will not meet the high standards of putting God first and following the commandments. Jesus adds that it is difficult, but not impossible, for a rich man to enter the kingdom.[81]

Jesus speaks in several places of the anguish that will be experienced by those who are not ushered into the kingdom.

In the explication of the Parable of the Sower he says, "As the weeds are pulled up and burned in the fire, so it will be at the end of the age...the angels...will weed out of his kingdom everything that causes sin and all who do evil. They will throw them into the fiery furnace, where there will be weeping and gnashing of teeth."[82]

In the Parable of the Talents, the man who has entrusted his servants with various talents called in the man with one talent who had buried it. In his anger at this servant the man had his talent taken from him and given to the one with ten talents. Then he was to be "throw[n] outside into the darkness, where there will be weeping and gnashing of teeth."[83]

The punishment for "goats" is harsh and swift. In the Parable of the Net they [the bad fish] are thrown into the fiery furnace with the same torment.[84] In the Parable of the Wedding Banquet the king sends his army to kill the invited guests who killed his servants.[85] When the sheep and goats are separated, the goats go to eternal punishment.[86]

Regret and anguish are too late to save us once we have continued along our own path, ignoring what Jesus taught. There is a standard. The consequences are harsh for those who don't meet it.

But—and this is a big BUT—the standard includes the love of God for us, the fulfillment of all our gifts and talents, forgiveness for the wrongs we have done if we do turn back to him, the satisfaction of serving others, along with the adventure of serving the Lord. Jesus is not asking us to be perfect, only to show our intention to love and faithfully follow him, to do that with our all, to "love the Lord your God with all your heart and with all your soul and with all your mind."[87]

The blessings of doing this are a peace which we cannot comprehend or know the source of, a living out of our purpose with the totality of who we are—the deep satisfaction of that; a feeling of connectedness with God at the deepest level; an assurance that no matter what happens we will be fine; a rich prayer life; a communion, mostly wordless, that passes between the Lord and us; a deep confidence that we are following God's will for us as we know it; and much, much more.

This is the "Good News" that Jesus taught. It is all that we humans hope to find in the material world where we never find any satisfaction, where we never will. The material world operates at the surface level of desire, but entry into the kingdom requires us to go way below the apparent desire to the deepest levels of life. It is there that the Lord meets us.

The kingdom is not the kind of place where you can straddle the fence, have one foot in and one foot out. You're either all in or all out. Every decision we make either takes us closer to the kingdom or further away from it. Once we're in the kingdom every decision we make keeps us there. It's just not possible to waiver there, because our lives are so intertwined with God's Spirit that we cannot do otherwise. We can set our intention to get into the kingdom, but in the end it is God who decides, not us. Jesus says that "many are invited, but few are chosen."[88] All we can do is prepare for the kingdom and wait for an invitation.

We've seen in Jesus's teachings that a high moral standard and a humility, like a little child dependent on his parents, is required before one enters the kingdom, along with a life dedicated to the Lord. The kingdom is egalitarian and righteous, where we live in the presence of God. More on this subject in Part II…

PART II: PREPARING TO LIVE IN THE KINGDOM

Jesus has left us lots of instructions about preparing to enter the kingdom. What is required most of all is a deep relationship with Christ/God/the Holy Spirit—because most of the preparations are done by the Divine transforming us from the inside out.

We cannot transform ourselves no matter how much we may want to change. We are too close to the subject, too attached to our own opinions and assumptions and expectations to be of much use in changing ourselves. If the goal were to stay in this earthly context, then our knowledge of it would be invaluable. However, since the goal is to be in this world but not *of* the world,[89] what we know of the world is not helpful at all. There are, however, things that we can do to keep us on track in our relationship with God—that's what we'll be addressing here in Part III.

Our primary contribution to our own transformation is our dedicated willingness and commitment to go wherever God would take us. In the chapters of Part III we'll explore the various challenges God will lead us through as he transforms us into people who can love God with all of ourselves, who can love our neighbors and ourselves.[90]

I muse to myself that God, in looking at the few who would follow him and the many who wouldn't, must have wanted sometimes to wipe the human race off the face of the Earth like he did in the story of the Noah and the flood. Surely, during Babylonian exile, the Roman Empire, the Crusades, the ravages of the Huns, the many slaughters of the Innocents, and recently in the Holocaust, the Cambodian and Rwandan massacres and others, he was tempted. But he has stuck by his Covenant with Noah to let us be and come to him of our own accord.

As I muse further about this, I think about how hard it is for one of us to surrender our life to him. Jesus himself objected at the last moment to his fate before going ahead to his crucifixion and death.[91] We who follow him, as a result, have his footprints to walk in and his instructions to follow, the opportunity not to imitate but to emulate. What a gift.

CHAPTER 1

Be Born of the Water and the Spirit

"I baptize you with water for repentance. But after me comes one who is more powerful than I, whose sandals I am not worthy to carry. He will baptize you with the Holy Spirit and fire."[92]

As John sees it, being baptized with water is to repent, to change the pattern of your life. But then Jesus talks of being "born of the water"[93]—read this as the rite of baptism or possibly being born of the womb of a woman—and of the Spirit. This signifies the emergence of the Indwelling Spirit within the person, of him being given his role of leadership over the person. The Indwelling Spirit comes forward over a long time of building a close, co-creative relationship with God, after the surrender of the person, when the person is being gifted with the fruit of the Spirit and when he or she is ready for the ultimate step into the kingdom.

Baptism to me is an outer act signifying a preparation for the inner transformation of the coming emergence of the Indwelling Spirit. It is the first step in the transformation of an ordinary person into a person of God, but along with the beliefs it is only the first step.

We can see this in the disciples who for the two years of Jesus's ministry are at his side every day absorbing his teaching and his love. They were dedicated to him: they left their homes, families, and occupations to follow him. But even with all that they were not yet ready to take on his ministry. At the Last Supper they heard about the Holy Spirit and how he would be their advocate and would help them remember every single word Jesus had taught them.[94] But it wasn't until after Jesus died, dropped in on them several times in their grieving, and then ascended into heaven that the Holy Spirit entered into them and instantly transformed them into effective ministers of Jesus's teachings.[95] Totally guided by the Indwelling Spirit they could speak and be heard in any language. They could heal. They went from an outer dedication to Jesus to an inner transformation that enabled them to do what he had done. Wow!

Paul, who was to spread Jesus's teachings along with the disciples, also had an inner transformation inspired by God. Within three days of encountering the Risen Jesus—who asked, "Why do you persecute me?"[96]—he turned his life around, but it was three more years before he started his ministry[97] and proceeded to spread the early church throughout the Mediterranean world to the Gentiles.

This inner transformation is what Jesus refers to in the passage in John 3:5-6: "Very truly I tell you no one can enter the kingdom of God unless they are born of the water and the Spirit. Flesh gives birth to flesh, but the Spirit gives birth to spirit."

Sometimes we see baptism as conferring protection on a baby, something done by anxious parents so that she will go straight to heaven in case she dies. Or as the promise of the parents and by extension their church to make sure the baby is raised to be a Christian. Or, in Baptist churches, as an affirmation of faith by the emergent adult, a young teen, a believer's baptism.

The water symbolizes a cleansing, a purification, the removal of what stands between the person and God. It is a symbol, a promise that must be lived into. That is where the baptism by the Spirit enters the equation and becomes the real baptism. One starts with the baptism by water and, then, through an ever-deepening relationship with Christ one lives into the Life of the Spirit, the life lived in, with, and for God. When the presence of the Indwelling Spirit becomes the driving force in the person, when she has finally surrendered everything to Christ, when he has given up all his human assumptions, expectations, and demands of life, then s/he has been "born of the Spirit."

What needs to occur in order for that to happen? If we think in the terms of the Beatitudes, the poor in spirit are those who are emptied of themselves[98] and are capable of being filled by the Holy Spirit. Until we are finally emptied of the problematic parts of our very human side or they are transformed, the divine within us cannot come forward.

This does not mean that we are to get rid of our human nature, but that the ego, the personality, and the self-preoccupation—all very human traits—come under the authority of the soul and the Spirit for us to born again in the Spirit. The more rebellious parts of ourselves are absorbed under the aegis of the soul. They have been loved into acceptance by the authority of the soul and Spirit.

The soul needs the hands and feet, the voice and the mind of our human selves to be effective in this world, to advance the kingdom. Those who are born of the Spirit have "married" their soul and spirit to their physical being (the ability to act) and to their mind and voice (the ability to speak). They now live in the kingdom as their own true selves, using their talents and gifts and challenges in the service of the Lord.

Part II of this book is about an evolution of consciousness of the kingdom within us. For most this is a slow transformation. For the disciples, the enormous change happened after two years in Jesus's company, hearing his teaching, seeing the healings and learning from how he was with people of all different kinds. For Paul, it was a three-day turnaround after his encounter with the risen Christ plus the three years it took for him to be ready to lead the Gentiles to Christ.

No matter how long it takes us, the purpose of this encounter with God is to live in the kingdom as we persist and are faithful. If we offer ourselves up for healing, if we shed all the acculturated things about us, stripping down to our natural selves, then we become the people we were created to be. More human than ever and yet living out the divine paradigm for us—that is the goal of this spiritual journey.

To be born of the Spirit is the first big step for us. The next one is this: To be prepared for the coming of the Lord. Just turn the page to Chapter 2...

CHAPTER 2

Be Prepared for an Invitation at Any Time

The second major thing that we can do in order to enter the kingdom is to be prepared, to anticipate the invitation and look out for the call, to not only be ready to accept the invitation, but also to have everything in place and even have the proper "clothes" to wear. These instructions are found in the Parables of the Wise and Foolish Virgins, the Wedding Banquet (in Matthew and a similar one in Luke), and the Prodigal Son.

The Parables of the Ten Virgins and the Wedding Banquet in Matthew

The most obvious call to be prepared is found in the Parable of the Wise and Foolish Virgins. The parable ends with this instruction: "Keep watch, because you do not know the day or the hour" that the bridegroom will come.[99] The wise virgins not only had their lamps with them while they awaited the bridegroom, they had plenty of oil for the lamps, too. They had made all the preparations needed. But the foolish ones only had their lamps. They tried to cadge oil from the wise virgins but were refused because then no one would have enough. So they had to go out to buy oil, thereby missing the arrival of the bridegroom. When they came back late, the doors were locked and the bridegroom said to their pleas to enter, "I do not know you."

Both the lamps and the oil are needed for entry into the kingdom. Think about that. What is it that makes our personal lamps light up? What is the oil that makes us glow from within?

For me the oil is prayer, an open communion with Christ, a truly back-and-forth, co-creative relationship in which I am known to Christ and he is known to me because of all the time we have spent together. The "oil" that the foolish virgins were missing then was the real, day-in-and-day-out experience of Christ that cannot be substituted for or acquired at the last minute. It is something honed over the years through time spent and attention given to the Other. Otherwise, how could Christ know us?

The other interesting aspect of the parable to me concerns the bridegroom and the virgins, i.e., one bridegroom, many virgins. Taking this to mean we are all virgins—both men and women—before Christ, the bridegroom, I think the parable is suggesting an innocence in how we are to approach him, a paring down of sophistication and worldliness and also a sexual innocence. After all, we've never before joined/wedded with the Divine principle, so we need to come as our most natural selves, divested of all but the person we were created to be, ready to fulfill the purpose of our creation in the service of the kingdom.

By using the wedding metaphor Jesus seems to suggest that love is the vehicle, love is the way, and love is the outcome of this joining. The only three things we need to bring to this wedding are 1) our true selves with the ego and personality firmly under the aegis of the soul and Spirit, 2) our light reflecting the light of God, and 3) the "oil" for the light, our experience in communion with the Lord. Then we are ready to join with Christ in the kingdom.

Another aspect of preparation is found in the Parable of the Wedding Banquet.[100] Here the kingdom of heaven is compared to a king who issued invitations to a wedding banquet for his son. None of the invited guests came; they refused. So the king told his servants to go out to the streets and "gather all the people they could find, the bad as well as the good." In this way they filled the hall.

When the king entered and saw that one guest was not wearing the proper wedding clothes, he ordered the servants to "throw him outside, into the darkness where there will be weeping and gnashing of teeth. For many are invited, but few are chosen."[101]

The king had been angry at the ones who had refused to come, but he wasted no more time on them. He had the servants gather an assortment of people from the street corners and then objected to the dress of one of the guests. Again, there is stress here on the timing, which is God's: We don't know when the invitation to be in the kingdom will come or who will be invited, so we must be ready at all times.

But…what is the proper dress? Everyone would have known what to wear to a wedding in those days as well as they do in ours. To ignore the proper dress would have been an insult. What is Jesus saying about the clothes, though? Is it just about being ready? What should we be clothed in?

I think this has to do with the fruit of the Spirit. A fruit is the end product of the planting or growing cycle. If we do not have a deep relationship with God that we have nurtured diligently, then we are not yet "clothed," that is, we have not been gifted with the "fruit of the Spirit,"[102] which is peace, joy, love, patience, gentleness, kindness, self-control, faithfulness, and goodness. When I think about these gifts I see them as one really, all under the banner of love. They are interdependent. How can we be loving if we don't have self-control or kindness or patience? How can we be at peace without love or joy or faithfulness? Each one consists of all the others. That is why in the passage quoted in Galatians the word "fruit" is singular, not plural.

If we haven't been given the fruit, we are still too full of ourselves and not emptied out to where the Spirit can fill us. We are not humble; we are still operating more out of the ego-self than the soul-self. The first guests to be invited refused to come. The next group, rounded up on a street corner, came; some were ready, one was not. Only the ones who were ready were welcome to stay.

The relationship that we help build with the Divine One is the essential preparation for the invitation. There are no shortcuts, no assuming a place for yourself if you haven't spent anywhere near enough time together. Otherwise, as in the Parable of the Wise and Foolish Virgins, the bridegroom will say, "I don't know you." You have to do the preparatory work of getting to know Christ and letting him know who you are in order to achieve a place in the kingdom.

The Parables of the Lost Sheep, the Lost Coin, and the Prodigal (Lost) Son

In Luke 15 Jesus tells a series of parables about the lost sheep, the lost coin, and then the lost son. In each story there is something that is lost, an all-out search or watching and waiting for its return, and great rejoicing when what's lost is found.

In the Parable of the Lost Sheep Jesus asks if we had a hundred sheep and one was lost, wouldn't we leave the 99 and go after the one who was lost? And when we came home carrying the sheep, wouldn't we celebrate his return? That is what happens in heaven when one sinner repents. Lost, found, and celebrated.[103]

This theme was echoed in the Parable of the Lost Coin: a widow who had 10 coins and lost one searches for the lost one until it is found. And she celebrates. As does heaven when one sinner repents.[104]

In the Parable of the Lost (or Prodigal) Son,[105] the son has spent all his inheritance and is now returning to his father's house, because, "when he came to his senses, he said, 'How many of my father's hired servants have food to spare, and here I am starving to death! I will set out and go back to my father and say to him: 'Father, I have sinned against heaven and against you. I am no longer worthy to be called your son; make me like one of your hired servants.'"[106] Now, the father has been keeping watch in case the son should come back, and when he sees him he runs out to greet him. He then restores his son to his rightful inheritance and place in the household and celebrates his return.

The son was not asking anything of his father other than to work for him and to eat and sleep like the servants did. But the father welcomes him back and celebrates the return of his lost son. The son has confessed all that he did that was wrong—has repented in Biblical terms—and has come back to make a fresh start. I imagine that he came back ashamed and maybe even afraid of how he would be received, but he is met with love and embraced and fully restored to his place in the family.

The implications for us in this parable are huge. No matter what we have done that was wasteful or sinful or "off the mark" as the Hebrew word that we translate as "sin" has it, we are welcomed with love once we have done a 180-degree turn away from those deeds and failures to act. We are human, inconstant, sometimes evil, sometimes good, but beings with divine potential.

The lost son is repenting, declaring that he is reformed; he has faced himself fully and seen all that he is and has done and he is not hiding any of it. He would be a servant in his father's house, just for the nourishment it would provide. And the father—read God—embraces him as he is, loves him, has missed him. Now the father can celebrate because what was lost to him is now found in him. And the "lost" son is restored to his inheritance. For me, this is the key testimony about the nature of our God and how he deals with our errant ways. Wow! It is the nature of the kingdom that God is always casting seed, hints and suggestions, lures and bait, invitations to attract us to his kingdom and to our inheritance as children of God. He puts the seeds right in our paths for us to see and ignore or to take up and plant in fertile soil in our hearts and minds so that we might embrace our natural inheritance as children of God.

Once we have been "born in the Spirit," though, there is a period of preparation, of building a true relationship with the Divine One, so that when he calls us into the kingdom, we will be ready to go. The parables of this chapter have shown us how to prepare.

In the Parable of the Wise and Foolish Virgins, we are told to be ready with our oil and lamps, because we don't know when the bridegroom will come.

In the Parable of the Wedding Banquet we are asked to come clothed in the right way and in the right spirit of humility. Obviously there is an A-list of invitees, the powerful, the rich who ignore the invitation or refuse to come. Everyone else drawn into the banquet are ones with no particular position or power in society that are invited at the last moment, humble people who get to revel in the banquet—much to their surprise, I suspect.

And then there are the stories of the sheep and coin, in which the lost thing was found and celebrated, and that of the lost son, who has repented of all he did to throw away his inheritance. He is welcomed with open arms and celebration, too.

If we were to summarize this chapter about preparation in a few words, they would be: prayer, humility, faithfulness, and repentance.

In the next chapter we will discuss treasuring God and the kingdom above all else.

CHAPTER 3

Treasure the Kingdom Above All Else

The Parables of the Hidden Treasure and the Fine Pearl

"Seek first his kingdom and his righteousness and all these things"—what to eat, what to wear, all your needs—"will be given to you as well. Therefore do not worry about tomorrow, for tomorrow will worry about itself."[107] This passage follows the one about the "flowers of the field."[108] Here we read the direct promise that if we put God and his kingdom first, then we will have no worries, that every single thing that we need will be provided to us. With our attention fixed on the kingdom, we are free, free to be and to do what we were created to do in this world, which I believe is to help bring in the kingdom, to make it visible, using our God-given gifts and talents and even our challenges.

Jesus offered us this rock-bottom principle of the Life of the Spirit: to put God and his kingdom first above all else in different ways in the Gospels. It is stated as a governing principle in the Parables of the Hidden Treasure and the Fine Pearl, as well as in the stories of two people who were headed to the kingdom, but one wanted to bury his father first and the other who wanted to say farewell to his family.

It is through a process of surrendering our lives to God, using spiritual practices to learn how to hear that "still, small voice" and then to follow its suggestions, making God the absolute priority in our lives, that we begin to serve and love God with all of ourselves as the main trajectory of our lives.

And finally there is a point when we cannot any longer identify with the world: we are securely, faithfully in God's arms. And nothing can dislodge us.

In loving God with our whole selves we are putting God and his kingdom first, we are giving ourselves to God and to others; we are not denying our own needs, but we know that God will take care of them so that they no longer need to preoccupy us.

Jesus certainly knew how great a hold the human culture has on us, so all of these examples he gives about treasure and not turning back once we decide on the kingdom are clear, nothing that needs interpretation. In the parables about the treasure in the field and the pearl of great price,[109] we see Jesus once again emphasizing the centrality of the kingdom in a life: "The kingdom is like treasure hidden in a field."[110] A man found it and buried it again. He then sold all his possessions and bought the field. It's interesting: he didn't steal it, which he could have done. He bought it with the proceeds of the sale of everything else he owned. He gave up everything; afterward he only possessed the treasure.

What did he have to give up? Any attachments he had to things or ways of thinking and being in this world, anything that did not put the kingdom first. "No other gods before me."[111] And what are the gods we put before God? It is an incredibly long list, different perhaps for each person. Here are some of mine, a list I developed after surrendering my life to Christ: other people's opinions of me, candy(I have a sugar addiction), my expectations of how my life should go, our culture's view of women, my fear and doubts, my assumptions about what works in life, preoccupation with how I look, and many, many more gods.

The importance of the treasure to the man cannot be overstated—he sold everything he had to obtain it. So he rightfully and lawfully put everything he had into buying the treasure. Wow! Again there is the inference that his needs will be met by his reverence for the treasure, for the kingdom. He has no more needs that will not be fulfilled.

In the Parable of the Pearl a merchant is searching for fine pearls. And when he found one of "great value,"[112] he sold everything he had and bought it. Again in this parable the emphasis is on buying the treasured pearl with the equivalent of all his possessions. He isn't bargaining for it. He doesn't steal it. He gives up everything to possess that pearl of great value. Jesus clearly restates here that the kingdom comes first above all possessions and, I would add, everything else we hold dear: our expectations, assumptions about life, and our preferences for how our lives should proceed and more.

He brings the point home more forcefully in the last two stories.[113] He had invited one man to "follow me,"[114] who had replied that he needed to bury his father first. Jesus tells him, "Let the dead bury their own dead, but you go and proclaim the kingdom of God." And who are the dead? People who no longer hold sway over the man? Things that don't matter any more?

Another man wants to say goodbye to his family first before he follows Jesus and Jesus replies, "No one who puts a hand to the plow and looks back is fit for service in the kingdom of God."[115]

To me there is a clear implication that the kingdom is all about life, maybe LIFE in all capitals, and that anything else is death. So when the first man wants to honor his father by burying him, he is choosing death over life, the past over the present. And when the second man wants to say goodbye to his family, he is also choosing the past over the present. If we are ready for the kingdom, if we put it first, then these issues have no meaning to us at least in the context of the kingdom, and we are choosing that context. We are ready to go or we are totally not ready.

To be ready with one's heart, mind, body, and soul to enter the kingdom is to have already released all attachments, to have prepared the people close to you that they no longer have any hold on you, in effect to have already said your goodbyes.

Remember that in other passages Jesus has said both "Honor your father and mother,"[116] but "anyone who loves their father or mother more than me is not worthy of me."[117] In these seemingly contradictory teachings Jesus is getting at the principle of putting God first above all—above all the people that we love, especially our parents and family, friends, the people we are closest to. They are to be secondary to us in loving God above all else. Their opinions, their assumptions about us, what they taught us, what they expect from us—all this is secondary to listening to God. We are to honor them, care for them, love them, but all of this we do in the context of being in God's kingdom and following his instructions for how we are to be with them. That is how we are to put God first.

The cost of following Jesus is high and harkens back to the last chapter on preparation. When we say yes to Jesus, when we surrender our lives, when we live out the thousands of surrenders along the way, when we finally have gotten to the place where the kingdom is first in our lives, there is no delay allowed, we are to be ready to be and to do what God has intended for us. No delay, no putting other people or things first, no denial or postponement, only faithfulness and dedication to the kingdom.

For God wants our all and nothing short of that will do. God needs us on the world stage, putting the kingdom first, using our talents and gifts and shortcomings all in the service of advancing the kingdom. This is what we've been designed for. And it is what following Jesus means: that we place our whole lives in his hands and follow, as Jesus did his, our destiny, still with our eyes on the kingdom and the King. We may have moments as he did in Gethsemane when he went back and forth between "if you are willing, take this cup from me" to "yet not my will but yours be done."[118] But then we are fulfilling our lives as he did, no matter the personal cost to us. From where we sit now, not quite close to where God will take us, we see only the cost, but on the cross Jesus clearly was seeing God and forgiving mankind. One moment again, he muttered these words, "my God, my God, why has thou forsaken me?"[119] And in the next moment he surrendered his spirit to God.

It is clear from these short parables and teachings that putting God and his kingdom first are high on the list of qualities needed to enter the kingdom of God. To obtain the treasure, to sell all that he has, to walk away from his dead father, to not say goodbye to his family, a man or woman has to be free of all encumbrances, all the past, all the worries, all that enslaves us.

There are a lot of verses in the Gospels where Jesus talks about the coming of the Son of Man.[120] And there are even more references in the Epistles and Revelations. We've already discussed the implications of the separation of the sheep and the goats, of the good fish and the bad fish. Here I just want to add that we bear some of the responsibility for the viability of the kingdom on earth, for its visibility in everything we do.

If we are living in the kingdom, we are contributing love, peace, joy, forgiveness, gentleness, kindness, faithfulness, self-control and patience to the world. We are modeling a wholly different way to live. We are the visible members of the kingdom. The sooner we get there and contribute to it, the sooner its effects will be felt all over the world. It is not just when Christ comes that the kingdom will be ushered in, but when enough of us who constitute the body of Christ can live in the kingdom with Christ . Then we will help realize the kingdom's coming.

In Chapter 4 we'll discuss using and multiplying our gifts and talents.

CHAPTER 4

Use Your Gifts, Let Them Multiply

Two parables carry this message: Use your gifts and talents, let them multiply.

The Parable of the Gold Bags (or Talents) and the Parable of the Ten Minas

The first parable is in Matthew.[121] A man went away for quite a while and before he left he entrusted three servants with some of his coins. To one he gave five, to a second he gave two, and to the third he gave one. The first two servants went right to work and doubled what the man had given them. The third buried his one coin because he was afraid of his master.

When the owner returned he celebrated the gains of the first two servants, but when he met with the third and heard that he had buried the coin out of fear of him, he was furious. At least, suggested the master, he could have earned some interest from the bankers. He gave the man's coin to the one who had ten and had the man thrown out into the darkness. In the NIV Bible this parable is called the Parable of the Gold Bags, but traditionally it has been called the Parable of the Talents.

The owner entrusted his servants with his coins—talents, gold, however you like to think of it. He trusted them with parts of his kingdom and he rewarded those that used their "talents" to double what he gave them. He trusted them and they repaid his trust. There is a clear statement here that we are to use whatever God has given us and to multiply them by investing them.

The third servant who feared the Lord and didn't trust him didn't use his coin to multiply its value or even to earn interest. He knew the owner as a "hard man," not as one who had his interests at heart. So he buried his coin, didn't even invest it with a banker where it would have earned some interest. He refused to participate in a positive outcome for the master and for himself.

In Luke's version, the Parable of the Ten Minas,[122] the man went to a distant country to get himself made king. Before he left he called ten of his servants and divided ten minas among them. "Put this money to work," he said, "until I come back." One mina was the equivalent of three month's wages.[123]

When the man returned, he asked his servants about the money. The first one said that his mina had gained ten more. The second had gained five more. And another servant brought back his coin and gave it to him. "I was afraid of you, because you are a hard man."[124] The man took his coin and gave it to the one with ten. When the other servants complained that he already had ten, the man replied, "I tell you that to everyone who has, more will be given, but as for the one who has nothing, even that they have will be taken away."[125]

There are two added elements in Luke's story.

First, this landowner wanted to be king of a distant country. Though it turned out that those subjects objected to him being their king, he nonetheless was made king. After he returns home he tells his servants to bring those who objected to his being king and to slay them in front of him.

Second, the servants were given one mina each. The one who earned ten minas was given charge of ten cities; the one who earned five minas was given charge over five cities.

Clearly, there is a loyalty issue here: Those who use his money wisely and multiply it and those who accept him as king are rewarded, but those who fear him or rebel against him are punished.

Jesus tells this parable, according to Luke, because the people near Jerusalem thought the kingdom was going to appear very soon.[126] In telling this story he seems to be saying that there is a waiting time of investment where everything can come into fruition before the kingdom can come. In a way it's like saying that each of us has to demonstrate our wise use of our talents (minas or gold or gifts) before the kingdom can come in us or we dwell in it. We have to invest ourselves in the growth of what we have been given, be wise stewards of the gifts we have.

If you follow athletics at all, you will notice that it is not always the most talented person who goes the farthest in his sport, but the one with the most determination and willingness to work hard to develop the talent he has. We are not given a free pass just because we have talent. We cannot rest on our laurels; we are asked in our lives to continue to invest what we've been given, what we have, so that we can give back to our Creator much more than we've been given.

In these two parables this lesson is made clear: It is what we do with what we've been given that is important, not how much we have. So whether we have five or two coins or one the same proportion of growth is expected.

I'm not sure what to make of situation of the man who would be king to the people in a distant land, but I expect it has to do with people's perception of that man. Like the servant who held onto or buried the coin he was given, they see him as a hard man. They have judged him from their own narrow perspective. He is a generous man with those who will work with him. But for those who fear him, who won't give him his place in their lives, he has no care. In Matthew he has the servant thrown out into the darkness. In Luke he takes away the coin he gave him, and then he has all the subjects in the distant land that objected to him killed. Do you hear the echo of the bridegroom's response to the foolish virgins, "I don't know you"? We haven't been working together. We don't communicate. We don't even agree on so many things. You were not ready for me. I don't know you.

To be known to the master/the owner/the bridegroom is to be in a deep relationship, to have given over one's life in service to the One, to have shared all that you are, all your pain and suffering, all the blessings and grace, to have walked a long way together. There are no barriers between you and him, he is your best friend, your companion, the one who challenges you to your best, the one who loves you, the one who knows you best.

This is the kind of relationship Jesus is talking about that defines who is in the kingdom and who is not. I don't know you and you really don't know me—maybe from what people have told you, from what you have read, but not from personal experience. What is truly valued in Jesus's teaching is your very own experience of the living God and using all that he has given you to give back to life, the needy, the grieving, the sick, the prisoner, the hungry, and the thirsty.[127]

I grew up in a hellfire-and-damnation church, so I can relate to the men who buried the coin in fear. But I think that what we were taught as children should never be the end of the story. Am I forever to think of God as punishing, vengeful, and capricious? Am I to continue to fear him? Do I bury all he has given me and not use it? Or do I continue to search for a way to love God?

To put it another way, do I seek out a God that I can live with, and then let God show me who he is? Our lives need to be built on our experience of God, not on the teachings about God. Those teachings, now incorporated in us as beliefs, can be very limiting or even harsh, as in my case, depending on the interpretation. The goal is to have a relationship, a deep one, with the living God, the living Christ, not with the one who is solidified or codified in our religions.

I know that this dependence on God rather than the church makes the church uneasy and frequently judgmental about what is happening in the life of one who knows God well. Think of how the church regarded saints in its past. It was not able to rein them; each was following God's spirit no matter where it took him or her, whether what he or she was doing agreed with church doctrine or not.

In Chapter 5 we will follow this thread of using our gifts and letting them multiply along with emptying ourselves.

CHAPTER 5

Be Empty of Yourself

In the Beatitudes there are several declarations that call for us to be empty of ourselves. In this chapter I will be referencing Cynthia Bourgeault's chapter on the Beatitudes in *The Wisdom Jesus*[128] and Jim Forrest's concept of the Beatitudes as a ladder in which each rung, each beatitude, is dependent on the one before it being achieved before moving on.[129]

The first beatitude is usually translated "poor in spirit,"[130] but Bourgeault proposes that we think of that as being empty of ourselves.[131] Generally we are full of ourselves, our preoccupations, our assumptions about life, and our expectations of how our lives should proceed—these are the lenses through which we view and judge reality. But these ways of thinking and proceeding greatly hamper our ability to see what is really before us; they muddy our vision, they reinforce our own peculiar point of view. In order to participate in the kingdom we must empty ourselves of all these things as well as anything else we're attached to (including our mother and father and everyone else dear to us), so that we can cleanly attach ourselves to God with all of ourselves—heart, mind, soul and body.

To empty doesn't necessarily mean to get rid of. In a spiritual context to be empty means to have nothing between us and God—no walls, no hidden agendas, or no hidden pain and suffering. All needs to be revealed to God and in that revealing we invite healing, the release of shame and guilt; the very walls that come between us and God are to come down. A central issue of the spiritual life is our worthiness to approach God just as we are, warts and all. It is not about trying to fix ourselves up or put on a mask that will hide our imperfections. We go before God as we truly are, as we were created to be, plus all our experiences and their effect on us here on earth, all the things that we have done and are.

Then God has some good raw material to work with—our created purpose, talents, challenges and gifts—along with the pain and suffering along the way and the attachments to the culture that keep us in this world. Now as we appear before him naked, empty, we are able to be transformed, to be made ready to live in the kingdom. Being empty is the first step.

Once we are empty the next rung on the ladder of the Beatitudes is "Blessed are they who mourn, for they shall be comforted."[132] God who accompanies us on our journeys through life whether we are aware of him or not is there in our grief to support, sustain, comfort, and help guide us. Our part of this step on the ladder is to grieve fully all the little and big losses of our lives, to register the toll those losses have taken. Mourning, according to Bourgeault, is "a brutal form of emptying,"[133] so that we can receive. If we don't adequately grieve, then we will always be filled with ourselves, our losses, our attachments. If we grieve fully, we are free to be filled again, filled with the Spirit of God.

The third Beatitude is "Blessed are the meek, for they shall inherit the earth."[134] To Bourgeault the meek are those who are "gentled."[135] Think of the difference between a horse which has been "broken" and a horse that has been gentled. Both horses are tame, but the first horse complies and the second one attaches himself to the trainer. It's the same with us humans. We can be broken, but there will always be an undertone of anger or rebelliousness. If we are gentled in our training, then we are the trainer's for life.

THY KINGDOM COME!

The last Beatitude, "Blessed are those who are persecuted because of righteousness, for theirs is the kingdom of heaven,"[136], refers to where we put God and his kingdom first above all. There is a story about Cyprian, the bishop of Carthage in North Africa in the 3rd century AD.[137] This was a time of many emperors in the Roman Empire, and some of them persecuted the Christians and some didn't. But in 258 AD the emperor Valerian issued a decree that all bishops, priests, and deacons who did not swear allegiance to him be put to death. Cyprian refused to swear allegiance. The governor of Carthage was reluctant to execute a member of his class, but Cyprian, thinking that he needed to be a martyr for the church, that it was his time, insisted that the execution take place. He, along with his followers, marched out to the place for the executions. He asked his followers to tip the executioner, because he was only doing his job. Then he stretched his hands out behind his back so that they could be bound. And he stretched his neck out for the executioner's blade. Many thousands converted to Christianity upon seeing or hearing of his courage and his lack of fear, his faith in God, in the face of death.

When a person has completed all the rungs of the ladder of the Beatitude, is empty, then radically emptied, gentled, merciful, pure in heart, peacemakers, and persecuted, she or he is so far beyond any care for her/his own life that s/he is only living in service to the kingdom. That is how the early martyrs like Cyprian faced their executioners—without fear or trembling. They no longer identified with this world, only with the kingdom which is here and now. Bourgeault calls this freedom.[138]

These martyrs and others who totally placed their trust in the Lord believed what Jesus taught: "Take my yoke upon you and learn from me, for I am gentle and humble in heart. And you will find rest for your souls. For my yoke is easy and my burden is light."[139] Free of all concerns. Free of fear of death. Free to face the persecution as Jesus did.

"For I am gentle and humble…" What is humility? Is it abasement, putting yourself down, especially putting down all that arises from the body? Is humility, as we have traditionally seen it, a cloak that hides our human nature? Where anger and fear and power peek out from under the cover? This is a false humility, one that has not been achieved, but is desired in the culture of a church. When I was growing up, people were sure to wear a cloak of piety and humility trying to outdo each other in abasing themselves.

This is not humility. It is a pretense. True humility in a religious sense is knowing one's place in the scheme of things—that one is second to God and the equal of every single human being on this planet, no matter one's education, job, place in the power structure, race, or religion. It is the lack of a need to be noticed, to call attention to oneself, to any longer be underhanded in gaining what one needs.

And further, and more importantly, humility reflects our awe of and reverence for God, for his providence, for meeting our needs, for the outcome, no matter what, that all will be all right. It's about walking this earth on holy ground, taking off our shoes before the burning bush.[140] Cyprian was a humble man. He wasn't thinking that as bishop he needed to live to guide his flock, that he was essential to the group. He gave himself up to what was needed at the time.

Jesus complained about the Pharisees and the teachers of the law because they were full of themselves: "They do not practice what they preach…everything they do is done for people to see…"[141] and much more. Then he spoke directly to the crowds and the disciples: "The greatest among you will be your servant. For those who exalt themselves will be humbled and those who humble themselves will be exalted."[142] We are to serve our Lord in other people and circumstances, not to be served. We can count on our own needs being met,[143] so we are freed to serve others.

Jesus in his last meal with his disciples begins by washing their feet. There is something about these smelly, dusty feet, calloused and dry feet, that tells more about Jesus' own humility than the humble act itself. Then he begins to teach them, "Do you understand what I have done for you? he asked them. "You call me 'Teacher' and 'Lord'" and rightly so, for that is what I am. Now that I, your Lord and Teacher, have washed your feet you also should wash one another's feet. I have set you an example that you should do as I have done for you. Very truly I tell you, no servant is greater than his master, nor is a messenger greater than the one who sent him. Now that you know these things, you will be blessed if you do them.'[144]

Then in Luke 22 in describing the last supper, Jesus interrupts a dispute among the disciples as to who is the greatest: "Instead, the greatest among you should be like the youngest, and the one who rules like the one who serves. For who is greater, the one who is at the table or the one who serves? Is it not the one who is at the table? But I am among you as one who serves."[145] Jesus does not trumpet his powers, his ability to heal. He doesn't claim to be the son of God; mostly he dodges those questions. He has come to serve, to teach, to heal, but not to proclaim an earthly kingdom with him as the king like David. He has come to serve!

Humility, service—these are the watchwords of Jesus. He did not play favorites with his disciples, did not encourage that kind of competition. He continually stressed service and he lived it, too. He personified humility—not self-abasement, but real awe and reverence for his Abba and service for all his fellow humans.

In Chapter 6 we'll be looking at the second of the Great Commandments: to love your neighbor as yourself.

CHAPTER 6

Love Your Neighbor as Yourself

The Second Great Commandment depends on the first one, which is to love God with all of ourselves—heart, mind, soul, and strength.[146] It is in the context of loving God, of putting the kingdom first, that we are then able to love ourselves and others. As we open ourselves to loving God, we have to also open up to loving ourselves. Our capacity to love depends on us doing that. For who can love who has never felt loved? Who can love who needs love most of all? Who can love who is hiding all that they are, out of fear of judgment or rejection? We must feel that we are lovable and loved before we will be able to take in God's love for us and then pour it out again to our neighbor.

And who is our neighbor? EVERYONE! Whoever is right before us. Whoever God asks us to serve. It's not only the person who lives next to us or our friends and family, people like us, but the stranger who calls us through God to serve him.

The Parable of the Good Samaritan

Jesus told the Parable of the Good Samaritan[147] in response to this question: "Who is my neighbor?"

On the way from Jerusalem to Jericho a man was set upon by robbers. He was left half dead. A priest crossed the road when he saw him and so did a Levite. But a Samaritan, when he saw the condition of the man, went to him, bandaged his wounds, and put him on his donkey to carry him to an inn. After caring for him that night he paid the innkeeper for his care and promised to return and pay any extra that he had incurred.

Jesus then asked the person who had asked the initial question, "Which of these three do you think was a neighbor to the man who fell into the hands of robbers?" And he replied, "The one who had mercy on him."[148] The "neighbor" in this case was someone who was unknown to the priest, the Levite, and the Samaritan. The priest and Levite crossed the road and went on their way, but the Samaritan had compassion for the one who had been badly hurt. It didn't matter who it was; he helped because help was needed.

What is mercy? The ancient Greek word translated as mercy in this passage is *eleos*, a noun. It meant "mercy, pity, the moral quality of feeling compassion and especially of showing kindness toward someone in need. This can refer to a human kindness and to God's kindness to humankind."[149]

Mercy, kindness, and compassion are all tied into the fruit of the Spirit: Mercy is part of love, as is compassion; kindness is part of love and patience and goodness. These are not distinct qualities we can acquire one by one. They are interdependent attitudes toward another person which are given to someone who has a deep, interdependent relationship with God. One cannot love if there is no compassion or kindness or goodness or patience or joy or self-control or any of the other fruit. They are not practiced by us so much as gifted from the depths of our soul, from God, in gratitude for our putting God first.

These qualities are the requirement for entrance into the kingdom. Nothing less will do, except we be loving, kind, patient, at peace, joyful, good, faithful, gentle, able to control ourselves[150]—all the fruit of the Spirit. I imagine on that first Pentecost Day suddenly the disciples were filled with the Spirit, experiencing an instant transformation into the ability to heal, to be heard by non-Hebrew speaking peoples of all languages. They were also filled with the fruit of the Spirit. The fruit of the Spirit was what they needed to carry on Christ's work on Earth then. And that fruit is exactly what we need to carry on Christ's work on Earth now.

One cannot show compassion without being loving; we can't be patient if we are not kind and so on.

Four times in Matthew's Parable of the Sheep and Goats Jesus cites these compassionate actions, twice in the positive sense and twice in the negative: "I was hungry and you gave me something to eat, I was thirsty and you gave me something to drink, I was a stranger and you invited me in, I needed clothes and you clothed me, I was sick and you looked after me, I was in prison and you came to visit me..."[151] He is really emphasizing helping those in need of food, drink, clothing, shelter, care, and visits. How much more specific could he be than to detail these basic needs? We are to fill the needs of anyone we see crying out for help.

In verse 40 Jesus again adds to the definition of neighbor: "Truly I tell you, whatever you did for one of the least of these brothers and sisters of mine, you did for me."[152] And here is the reason why we are to be so helpful to our neighbors, be they strangers or next door to us: We are to see Jesus in the face of the person who is in need; we are to respond to him or her as if Jesus was standing right before us. Each and every person no matter their race or religion or circumstances of life has the Indwelling Spirit of God (whether or not it is realized), was created by our Lord in God's image, and is deserving of our help and attention.

If we are in an intimate relationship with God/Christ Jesus/ Holy Spirit, then we are to treat every single person as if the one we worship is standing right in front of us. And what are we to do with God in all his guises? To love him with all of ourselves. And so with the neighbor as with God. For in this moment the neighbor is the closest being we have to God standing right before us with his needs. And we are to fill them using all the love and compassion and joy and patience and peace and the other fruit of the Spirit that we have within us.

Love is the currency of the kingdom along with all the other fruit of the Spirit. Without God's love and our own, we are lost. God's perfect love is the great change agent of this world: Anyone who experiences it cannot stay the same. So if we bring God's love to everyone we encounter, if we are living examples of the fruit of the Spirit, we are unleashing the power of love to transform and correct, to heal and to bind.

In Chapter 7 we will look at entering the kingdom as a little child.

CHAPTER 7

Be as a Little Child

Jesus welcomed the little children after his disciples tried to turn them away, for "the kingdom of heaven belongs to such as these."[153] Why would Jesus say that? Little children aren't yet of a reasonable age; they are dependent on parents to fill their needs; they can't leave home and follow him. So what did he mean here?

Little children and babies…don't really know how to fill their needs. They might be hungry, but they need a wise parent to provide a meal of healthy choices in order to get the right nutrition. Or they don't recognize danger when it comes—they might run into the road without looking. They need someone to guide their behavior. It takes a long time to grow up a child to make the wise and healthy decisions of an adult. And some adults never get there.

So what is it about little children that qualifies them for the kingdom of God?

First, they have a lot of needs for food, shelter, and clothing that someone wiser than they are has to fulfill. So they are dependent on someone else.

Second, they need to be loved. If we watch children at all different ages, we can see that once their physical needs are met they need to be loved, embraced, seen in all their glory and in their struggles to learn how to behave in this world. When children are trying out a new trick, telling a joke, or doing almost anything, they have an eagle eye out to see if a parent or grandparent or friend will notice and celebrate or commiserate with them.

They're looking to see if someone is really on their side. Someone who provides love, acceptance, meets physical needs, bandages hurts, and acknowledges hurt feelings. Someone to provide guidance about how to handle life.

Jesus says we are to "receive the kingdom of God like a little child." Obviously he is not talking here about going back to crawling on the floor. What *is* he talking about?

Jesus promises that just as a child can rely on his/her parents to fill all his/her needs to take care of and teach him/her we can be sure that our needs for food, clothing, shelter, purpose, and meaningful life will be met—because "your father knows that you need them. But seek his kingdom, and these things will be given to you as well."[154] The relationship he describes could be seen as a totally dependent one, but to me it feels more like a pilot–co-pilot relationship. As I co-pilot with God the "airplane" that is my life, there is a lot of back-and-forth between the two of us, a conversation in which I describe all that is on my heart and mind, we talk it over, I do a lot of listening, and then I follow his lead—because he knows so much better than I do what I really need, what the next step on the journey is that I need to take. I am way too close to my life to sort that out for myself. I am learning to fly, to live, but the wheel is firmly in his hands.

The other thing about little children is their innocence. They are not jaded. They have not tried out everything, even the things they shouldn't be doing. They are not sophisticated. Whatever they are feeling, everyone around them will know immediately. There is no artifice; nothing is hidden. They have integrity as few adults do.

So here is when we go back to the innocence of a little child: we strip off the layers of sophistication, disobedience, and cultural and even family conditioning until we come back to the self that we were created to be, to the raw material that can be shaped and formed as God see us and wants us to be. Now finally the soul/Spirit is in charge, not the personality or ego; it has been encompassed, eclipsed by the soul. The soul holds the agenda for our lives that God implanted in us at conception, and in conjunction with the Holy Spirit it will lead us where we were long ago meant to go. God has a purpose in mind for each of us. It entails using our gifts and talents and even challenges to love and to bring in the kingdom here on earth.

If all our needs are being met by God, what does that mean for us? Since we can count on God to meet our physical, spiritual, psychological, and mental needs, we are free! We are free to express who we are in the world. We are free of all economic restraints. We are free of others' expectations for us. We are free to be exactly who we were created to be. And in this dependent relationship with God, since we are greatly loved, we are able to love greatly, to let God's love flow in and out of us to everyone we meet. Along with love we are freely giving out patience, joy, peace, goodness, kindness, gentleness, faithfulness, and self-control—the fruit of the Spirit.

When we can freely give of God's love to everyone we meet, when we have been gifted with the fruit of the Spirit because of our deep relationship with and dependence on God, then we are doing what we were created to do in this world with love. And the ability to love like God loves is what brings in the kingdom. For this everlasting, ever-flowing, undiscriminating love is the great change agent of the world. It is the currency of the kingdom and everyone who changes from the world's view to God's view will find themselves in the kingdom.

In what I have written about all our needs being met there are echoes of the Great Commandment of Jesus to love God with all of ourselves—heart, mind, soul and strength.[155] For when our needs are met, when there is nothing lacking, when our hearts, minds, souls, and bodies are at peace, we then are able to love with all of ourselves. We then can love God, ourselves, and others. We can be present to God, ourselves, and others no matter what is going on. We can bring the fruit of the Spirit into any encounter and the other person feels the eternal love.

That is the goal of life here on Earth. It is as if God is asking us at every turn: Can you love when your world is falling apart? Can you love when things are going well? Can you love when you are sick, poor, infirm? If you are like a child in the arms of God, you can.

Innocence, dependence, seeking for needs to be met and love…these are the qualities of a little child that get us into the kingdom.

In Chapter 8 we address the all-encompassing First Great Commandment: to love God with all of ourselves.

CHAPTER 8

Love God With All of Yourself

Above all the requirements for getting into the kingdom is this one: to love God with all of ourselves—mind, soul, heart, and body.[156] This is the Great Commandment that Jesus proclaimed. It sums up all the other requirements, laws, and teachings in the Old Testament and the New. We are to bring our whole selves to God in love, worship, adoration, gratitude, need, and service. We are to be willing to go where God would take us and be willing to do what he asks us to do. We have to set our lives, our intentions upon serving him above all else, and in that process we have to lay down our weapons, our angers, fears, walls that separate us, expectations, assumptions, and wishes so that God can transform these enervating energies into creative, positive energy in service of his kingdom.

It took several years for the disciples and Paul to achieve this, but it can take a lifetime; that really doesn't matter. It's our readiness to serve, to put ourselves totally in his hands that matters. Like the workers in the vineyard, it doesn't matter if we start out in the morning or come in the last hour, the benefits are the same. No one is ahead of anyone else.

As we bring our whole selves to God we are shedding shame and guilt through God's transforming Spirit; they have no commerce in the kingdom. There everything is healed, everything about us is welcome. We are what we are. And, strangely enough in the kingdom, that is just fine. The kingdom isn't a place for perfect people, ancient and modern, who follow all the rules perfectly. We each bring our gifts and talents and challenges to the kingdom and all are welcome, because everyone and everything is used in the service of God.

Think how much lighter and freer we will be.[157] The expectations that we assumed in childhood have burdened us greatly and caused us much anxiety as we tried to fit into a one-size-fits-all cultural mold. When we realize that those conditions have ceased to work for us, when we are ready to lay those burdens down, we can shed all the conditioning we picked up in our families, through our friends, in our schools, and in the culture—everything that has nothing to do with who we really are. We are talking about freedom here, the very real freedom to be what you were created to be, using all that you are in the service of the Lord.

And who is this God we would serve with our whole selves? Our God is the Creator of the whole universe and maybe even multiple universes, as cosmologists are postulating today. He is the Designer of the incredible, intricate system in which all life sustains each other. He is Love and all that Love entails: embrace, patience, joy, participation, forgiveness, presence, and the desire to be together. No matter how mysterious and incomprehensible God is, he desires to know us each intimately, to guide and nurture us, to comfort and hold us, to be present to us. And when we are sincere in approaching him after doing a 180-degree turn on our very human behavior, he is like the father of the prodigal son or daughter who runs out to greet us, who throws a great celebration, and who restores us to our rightful inheritance.[158] Infinite and intimate. All-powerful and yet giving us free will and letting us recreate the world. Complex to the nth degree and yet able to be with us where we are. Creator and Caretaker of his creation. Brilliant and yet able to shade his light so he won't blind us. God is the great paradox of the universe. Knowable and unknown. Wow!

In the first of the two Great Commandments[159] Jesus directs us to love God with all of ourselves—heart, soul, and mind. In Mark's version he adds strength to these three,[160] which I read as our physical body. So Jesus is calling us to bring our whole selves to loving God. This is no small task. It is the main adventure/challenge of the Life of the Spirit to empty ourselves of the small self, so that God can fill us with love—love for God, ourselves, and for our neighbor. It is not that we get rid of parts of ourselves that aren't loving God, it's that we embrace them, shower them with love, transform them, and bring them under the aegis of the soul, where they are loved into conforming with the desire to love God with all.

Each chapter of Part III has described part of what it means to love God with all of ourselves: be born of the Spirit, be prepared, treasure the kingdom, use your gifts and talents, empty yourself, love your neighbor as yourself, be a little child with God.

*We cannot be born of the Spirit partially; we have to bring the whole of ourselves. *Our preparations can't be haphazard or incomplete; we need to be ready at all times for his call.

*We need to treasure everything—our lives, Jesus's teaching, God's presence, our calling, the Spirit's indwelling, and put these things above all else in our lives.

*We need to use what God has given us in our creation to multiply the gifts' and talents' affects, all in the context of our challenges. We are not to hoard or to fear God's punishment; we are to use our lives in service to God and to the Christ within all of us. *We are to be empty of our preoccupation with self, able to learn and grow and be freely in God's hands.

*We need to love our neighbors completely, helping them where we can, loving them as God has loved us.

*We need to come to God as little children, dependent, trusting, wide-open.

PATRICIA SAID ADAMS

*All of these intentions, gestures, attitudes help us bring our all to God—which is what Jesus asked of us.

PART III: CONCLUSIONS

The Agora

Imagine that you are visiting ancient Greece and you join in the daily walk to the *agora*, the marketplace, the center of Athens. It's all men (I can't help it, it's ancient Greece!)—citizens in good-standing—who gather every day. They belong to the army, they are merchants, they are philosophers and mathematicians, farmers and more. In the 5th and 4th centuries B.C. Athens was a democracy. It had ten tribes with representatives of each tribe helping to rule the city-state. Let's look at the attributes of the *agora*. It's a gathering place, a place where the government communicates to its citizenry, where they meet each other. For the men who gather here there is a sense of belonging, of solidarity. Ideas and goods are exchanged—it's Greece after all! There's inspiration, comradeship, solidarity, identity.

The *agora* is the image I was given of the kingdom, but the kingdom is more inclusive than the ancient *agora*—men, women, strangers, children even, people of all races, slaves and free, of all backgrounds. The kingdom is a state of mind more than a place, the gathering place for God's people, where love and mercy are the currency, where needs are met, where we are present to one another and to the presence of God, where everyone is a giver and a receiver, where no one stands above another for any reason. It's a place where everyone's gifts are honored and needed.

Imagine being in that marketplace. It's not an orderly, ideal place. It's loud and often boisterous. Joy breaks out as people see each other. Sometimes there's sadness in the news someone has brought. It's welcoming, though, to everyone. There is a warmth and sense of belonging that everyone can feel. There is time and energy to be with each other. It is a safe place where there is trust of each other, a place to hear all the news—sufferings as well as joy. There are jokes and pats on the back. There is inspiration shared. This is the realm of the Holy Spirit, who creates and inspires and loves and supports. Language, nationality are no longer barriers. And it is a very human place where all our foibles and sufferings are also welcomed. Here we are the whole people of God, the whole church of Jesus Christ.

As in ancient Greece there is purpose in all these interactions, purpose in coming to the gathering place of those who love and serve God and each other. There is a sense of anticipation, of expectancy, as each one awaits the Lord's next word in his/her life: what to do and with whom and how. There is movement as people gather around this person or that, as they greet each other, even strangers—for here even strangers are recognized and loved. Everyone feels at home, everyone belongs.

There is connection, belonging, connectedness not just to each other but to all of creation—the creatures and the plants, the winds and the rain, the sun and the moon, the beauty of it all. There is soul and soulfulness, a deep sense of each other, a willingness to put one's whole self into one's work and interactions. There is no distraction here, only presence, only love. There is no sense that the clock is ticking away the hours, but the sense that time, at least this moment and the next, is eternal. There is expansiveness, boundlessness.

There is God in Spirit whose love flows into and among and out of each person and group. There is a palpable sense of his presence. There is God who designed the whole system of the universe, who designed each and every person and soul here with purpose and meaning and desire, who desires that each person realize his or her full potential and give back to God and to the kingdom as he or she has been given to, in order to help realize the kingdom on this earth.

There is peace and love and joy and forbearance, kindness and goodness and faithfulness, gentleness and self-control—the fruit of the Spirit—all well established in those who gather here. The fruit is embedded in the connective tissue of the universe which is God's Spirit; the fruit is love in all its aspects, as God is love which binds us all together.

Unlike the *agora*, the kingdom is not a place; it is a state of heart and mind. It is a home for those of us who are in this world, but not of the world. It is not a place for perfect people, only for those who would bring their whole selves to God in love. It is the wheat among the tares until the harvest,[161] coexisting like a parallel universe right next to what we consider the "real world." Those who carry the kingdom in their hearts and minds bring it with them wherever they go. There is challenge and even suffering, but no one is ever alone: God is walking through life with us every step of the way, and then we have these companions, others who now live in the kingdom, along the way.

Think how different this is from the traditional view of the kingdom which I described in the Introduction to this book; it is not heaven, a place we go to after we die if we've perfectly followed God's law. The kingdom is a dynamic, not rule-bound place, because once Christ is firmly implanted in a person, that person cannot disobey the law. It is not even a concern.

The kingdom is a living, breathing place where we can dwell in freedom and love. It is home most of all, for those of us who live in the kingdom, a true home where we are always welcome where we are fulfilled by living out our purpose.

When we talk about dwelling in the kingdom, we're talking about bringing our whole selves to God—"the good, the bad, and the ugly" as the old Western movie title says. This is the fee for entry into the kingdom, you could say—entering the kingdom takes all of ourselves, warts and all; we are not to reject any part of ourselves. This echoes Jesus's great commandment: to love God with all of ourselves—heart, soul, mind and body (strength).[162]

Parenthetically, I'll add that I believe it is to the extent that we can love ourselves that we can love God and others. Here is my reasoning:

When we reject problematic parts of ourselves, we build walls around them so that we don't have to see them. We are hoping that they will disappear if we "forget" about them. Actually the reverse is true: What is denied is given more power over us. These barriers that wall off our less desirable selves wall us off not only from ourselves and others but also from God, in effect separating a good part of ourselves from God and severely limiting our relationship with God. In doing this we violate the Great Commandment of Jesus even as we are saying we love God. Maybe that is why we have chosen to see heaven as the perfect place where only perfect people dwell; it justifies a truncated relationship with God.

Here is how God who created us sees us: as whole, complete people, warts and all. He loves us, all of us. He gave us free will; he has always known how we would behave and yet he is always "sowing the seed,"[163] throwing out invitations to us, invitations which might land on rocky, clay-hard soil or among the thorns or sometimes on good soil, hoping to entice us to take a bite of his view of us, his word, his hope for us.

As we've seen in Part III in the Parable of the Prodigal Son,[164] both the prodigal son and the "good" son have missed the right relationship with their father. The first leaves home, rebels, spends all his inheritance. And the second one is caught in the dynamic of following the rules and never connects with his father's love. Both need to repair the relationship with their father.

The kingdom is filled with whole people who acknowledge their deficiencies, who live as close to their purpose as they can, who love God with as much of their selves as they can. To live in the kingdom takes a deep relationship with Christ, or as Paul puts it, "but we have the mind of Christ.[165] **The kingdom is the place where we can be real, where we can fully rest, it is the only real home for us.**

It is my contention that God has a specific purpose in mind for each of us in our unique creation that, if lived, will bring in the kingdom alive and visible on this earth. God needs each of us on the world's stage, doing what we were created to do and to be, each of us adding our voice to the chorus of people who can love and follow the Lord. I think that we've misinterpreted the passages of the Bible that speak of the second coming to mean that Christ alone will save the believers and judge everyone else. Could it be that Christ awaits enough men and women who will live his Gospel truths, who will love like he loves, before he comes again? If you were Christ, God and the Holy Spirit, wouldn't you want to see enough real people alive with your love to prove what Jesus taught, to concretize, realize the Gospel here on Earth?

This, to me, is the purpose of the church, the one body of Christ: to make real the song, "They will know we are Christians by our love, by our love." I'm afraid that the church is a far cry from living these lyrics, with fellow church members not respecting and loving each other, with denominations fighting and not embracing each other, with us not living the radical nature of Jesus's teaching, only a watered-down version in which we think we look good, but others can see the hypocrite in us.

No longer are we to think of the kingdom as distant, only to be accessed after death, but as a real, vital "place," an alternative to the world as we see it, as real as the world we know, but existing under different laws. The kingdom is in the here and now, as close to each of us as our breath and just as accessible, *if we are willing to abide in God and to follow his leadings for us*. He would evoke in us the capacity to love, and when we can love—embrace, accept, forgive, be patient with, be kind to ourselves and all others—then we will find ourselves living in the kingdom.

There is little we can do by ourselves that will gain us entry into the kingdom of God. Only by putting ourselves in the hands of the Holy Spirit and by our continued dedication to a deep and sustaining relationship with God can we be transformed by the Holy Spirit into people who, without reservation, serve the Lord. Then, in the kingdom, we will no longer be seeking a feel-good place, a perfect place, but a do-good-with-the-spirit-of-love place.

The Call

If you're waiting around for heaven after you die, then this message is not for you. If you think it is up to Christ alone to bring in the kingdom or the Second Coming, then you can quit reading now.

For the kingdom to become visible in this world, to be a viable alternative for many people, some of us Christians need to start living there right now, to demonstrate the freedom, the caring, the treasure of kingdom living. Christ is calling all of us—calling *you*— now. Will you answer, "YES!" and follow his lead? Will you seek out the depth of relationship with Christ that will gift you with the fruit of the Spirit? Will you work with love to make the kingdom real in this world? Will you make the Lord's prayer—"Thy kingdom come!"—a reality on this earth? Would you be one of a thousand, say? Or one of ten thousand people who can love? Or one of hundreds of thousands? Will you help make the kingdom a reality to this generation?

All the passages I have referred to in this book about Jesus's teachings about the kingdom are just information, somewhat interesting, if we don't take them seriously, if we don't see them applying to us, to our lives or to our relationship with God. The call will fall on deaf ears as it has for two thousand years. If we are complacent, if we feel that we have the right relationship with God, what I have written here will not provide any motivation for anything new to happen in our lives.

We can go on until we die living the way we do, we can keep going to church, doing "good works," all basically disconnected from the radical call of Jesus. We can call ourselves Christian and never put ourselves or our lives in Christ's hands. We can go unchanging through our lives, satisfied with what we have and who we are.

But there is a call in all that I have written about, a call for all of us, to hear and to heed, a call to move out of complacency, to make room for Christ in our lives, to put on the mind of Christ, to fulfill our purpose, to bring in the kingdom right here, right now on this earth. We need to move out of our comfortable lives which are mainly Earthbound and invite Christ into our lives, to transform us into people who can love, who can live in the kingdom.

In every passage of the Bible a call is put out to whoever has ears to hear and eyes to see. There is an invitation in Jesus's life to live as abundantly as he did with his eyes firmly fixed on the Father and his will. There is an invitation in his teachings—from the Sermon on the Mount to the way he went to the cross—to learn from him how to truly live.

God invites, hints, suggests, draws us to our true lives as we are created to be, to live out the purpose that he intended for us. He does not punish us if we don't. He doesn't cajole us. He leaves us to deal with the consequences. If we will, seriously and with dedication, answer his call, he will take us all the way to our created purpose, which is to bring in the kingdom of God here on this earth in the way implied by our gifts and talents. When we can be true to our purpose, when we can act with love wherever we go and in whatever we do, then we are bringing in the kingdom just by how we are in the world. It is the ability to love like God loves that makes the difference.

Only God can take the raw material of who we are today, the mistakes we've made, the sufferings that we've endured, the person we were created to be, and transform us into people who can truly love. Bit by bit he heals the parts of us that we offer up to him. Step by step he trains us to hone our skills. Gradually, as we offer up more and more of ourselves, as we learn to truly trust God and his providence for us, we become what he intended for us at our creation.

At some point in this process of a deepening relationship with God, we will be gifted with the fruit of the Spirit, so that we will truly be able to love, to take joy in, to have patience with, to be at peace with, to be gentle, kind and good to, to be faithful to and to have self-control[166] with everyone we encounter.

These are not qualities that we in any way can acquire on our own. They are the fruit, the end product of a growth process, a ripening dependence on, a growing love for and trust in God.

Having been gifted with the fruit of the Spirit, exhibiting it in all that we do and say, we are entered into the kingdom. Whatever we do, we do with love. Who we are becomes a demonstration of love in this world, just like Jesus's life was a demonstration of love in his world. We are now able to form a community, a true community of equals, of ones who have the same dedication, where everyone belongs, where everyone's gifts are essential.

This is the picture of the agora. It is a dynamic meeting place of equals before God. It is a place of the exchange of information, stories and inspiration, of holding his suffering, of honoring where she is, of sharing one's own humanity. It is not a perfect place; it is a place where the Divine rules over very human people, the whole people of God.

The kingdom is the church, the whole body of those who are living out their human and divine nature, but with their lives clearly focused on the Lord. They are truly in this world, but not of the world.

So…do you hear the call in this book, in these words? Will you answer the call with a resounding "YES!" Will you be one of those who will bring in the kingdom? Who will make the words we pray every Sunday—"Thy Kingdom Come!"—true and real on this earth? Will you surrender your life to God and let him lead you where he wants to take you? Will you then surrender every day your assumptions, expectations, and desires about how the world should be to embrace how it is right now in your life? Will you put God first above all else?

PATRICIA SAID ADAMS

Here's how the German poet Rainer Maria Rilke describes what stands between us and the kingdom:

> Between us there is but a narrow wall,
>
> and by sheer chance; for it would take
>
> merely a call from your lips or from mine
>
> to break it down,
>
> and that without a sound.
>
> The wall is builded of your images.
>
> They stand before you hiding you like names...[167]

Be the kingdom. Live your purpose. Be true to yourself and to your God. NOW!

ABOUT THE AUTHOR, PATRICIA SAID ADAMS:

I am a spiritual director and blogger about living the life that Jesus taught. I am not a theologian or a minister, so that the lens through which I view the kingdom is this: how do I, how do we, live this life centered in Christ? How do we build a relationship with Christ so that the Indwelling Spirit can transform us and help us realize our created purpose here on this Earth? My blog is at my website, **patsaidadams.com**, with ideas for spiritual practices at **deepeningyourfaith.com** and on YouTube at By the Waters by Pat Adams. I've written three other books, Called to Help the Poor and Needy, A Study Guide to the Beatitudes and the Sermon on the Mount, and Exodus: Our Story, Too! I live in Matthews, North Carolina.

Endnotes

1. Matthew 5:48
2. Strong's # 5455(Adj.), 5456(n.), 5457(v.), 5458(adv.), p. 1596, Teleios is the adjective form of the word meaning perfect in terms of completeness or fulfillment in the ancient Greek.
3. Matthew 6:28
4. Luke 15:11-32
5. Luke 4:18-9
6. Matthew 3:2 KJV
7. Matthew 3:2 NIV
8. Luke 17:21 KJV
9. Luke 17:21 NIV
10. Luke 17:21 NLT
11. Matthew 13:33 NIV
12. Jesus's contemporaries might have been shocked at his metaphor of the yeast throughout the baked bread. Yeast was a symbol of corruption in his world. (http://www.bibletools.org/index.cfm/fuseaction/Topical.show/RTD/cgg/ID/1559/Leaven-as-Symbol.htm) Again, the corruption was not obvious, but all the same determinative of the shape and nature of the society at the time.
13. Jesus often said that those who have eyes let them see and those who have ears let them hear. Mark 8:18 is one instance.
14. See the Final Discourses in John, Chapters 14-17
15. Matthew 4:19, 16:24, Mark 1:17, 8:34-5, John 14:6 for a few examples
16. John 15:9-17
17. John 18:36
18. Matthew 13:31-2
19. Matthew 6:28-34
20. Matthew 13:1-9
21. Matthew 13:24-30
22. The NIV Study Bible, Grand Rapids Michigan, Zondervan, 1985, p. 1461
23. Matthew 13:47-50
24. Matthew 7:16, 18
25. Genesis 9 8 Then God said to Noah and to his sons with him: 9 "I now establish my covenant with you and with your descendants after you 10 and with every living creature that was with you—the birds, the livestock and all the wild animals, all those that came out of the ark with you—every living creature on earth… 11 I establish my covenant with you: Never again will all life be destroyed by the waters of a flood; never again will there be a flood to destroy the earth." 13 "I have set my rainbow in the clouds, and it will be the sign of the covenant between me and the earth."
26. Mark 4:26-29

27 Matthew 7:13-4
28 Matthew 6:26-28
29 Luke 15:11-32
30 Luke 15: 31-2
31 Galatians 5:22-23
32 Matthew 20:1-16
33 Matthew 20:15-16
34 Galatians 3:28
35 Matthew 18:21-35
36 Luke 6:31
37 https://www.workingpreacher.org/preaching.aspx?commentary_id=1040, 6.15.15
38 Zondervan NIV Exhaustive Concordance, Strong's 1324, p. 1539
39 http://www.jesus.org/life-of-jesus/parables/what-does-the-unmerciful-servant-teach-us.html, 6.12.15
40 Matthew 8:12, speaking to the centurion; 13:42, explanation to the Parable of the Weeds; 13:50, the Parable of the Net; 22:13, the Parable of the Wedding Banquet; 24:51, the Parable of the Wise and Foolish Virgins/"the day and hour unknown"; and 25:30, the Parable of the Talents.
41 Luke 13:28 — "There will be weeping there, and gnashing of teeth, when you see Abraham, Isaac, and Jacob and all the prophets in the kingdom of God, but you yourselves thrown out."
42 Along with the New Testament book Revelation.
43 "From thence he [Jesus Christ] shall come to judge the quick and the dead." Nicene Creed of 325 CE. www.newworldencyclopedia.org/entry/Nicene_Creed#The_original_Nicene_Creed_ of_325, 9/5/11.
44 See the http://en.wikipedia.org/wiki/Second_Coming_of_Christ to learn more about leaders and sects through the ages who have made predictions about the second coming of Christ. Accessed 9/5/11.
45 Matthew 4:19
46 Matthew 13:47-50
47 Matthew 13:24-30
48 Zondervan NIV Exhaustive Concordance, Strong's # 4911, p. 1590
49 Matthew 13:36-43
50 Matthew 13:41-2
51 Matthew 6:33
52 Mark 12:28-31
53 Matthew 25:31-46
54 In addition, in the tradition of the Old Testament goats bore the sins of the Hebrews as scapegoats, the ones who carried the sins of the people and were sacrificed in place of a human being.
55 Matthew 25:36

56 Matthew 21:31 — Who are these "sheep" are who are welcome in the kingdom? In the temple courts Jesus calls out tax collectors and prostitutes for a place in the kingdom because they believed when many did not.
57 Matthew 21:43 — Who are some of the "goats" he is talking about? While he also proclaims that those who produce fruit would be in the kingdom, Jesus says that those in his audience, the chief priests and Pharisees, would not.
58 Matthew 22:1-14
59 Matthew 5:3
60 Matthew 5:10
61 Zondervan NIV Exhaustive Concordance, p. 1542, Strong's #1466. The Greek word for righteousness is dikaiosyne, which means doing what agrees "with God's standards" and "being in proper relationship with God."
62 Matthew 5:19-20
63 Ibid.
64 Matthew 6:33
65 Matthew 7:21
66 Matthew 13:11-2
67 Matthew 8:11-2
68 Matthew 19:14
69 Matthew 18:2-4
70 In Part III we'll address more of our part in entering the kingdom.
71 Matthew 25:1-13
72 Matthew 25:14-30
73 Matthew 20:1-16
74 Matthew 13:47-50
75 Matthew 13:24-25
76 Matthew 18:32-33
77 Matthew 23:13-4
78 Matthew 13:24-26
79 Matthew 5:19
80 Matthew 13:37-9
81 Matthew 19:23-4
82 Matthew 13:40-2
83 Matthew 25:30
84 Matthew 13:50
85 Matthew 22:6-7
86 Matthew 25:46
87 Matthew 22:37
88 Matthew 22:14, the end of the Parable of the Wedding Banquet
89 John 15:19
90 Mark 12:28-31
91 Matthew 26:36-46

92	Matthew 3:11ff
93	John 3:5
94	John 14:26
95	Acts 2
96	Acts 26:12, 15-16
97	Galatians 1:18
98	Cynthia Bourgeault, The Wisdom Jesus, Shambala, Boston and London, 2008 pps. 42-3
99	Matthew 25:1-13
100	Matthew 22:1-14
101	Matthew 22:13-14
102	Galatians 5:22-23
103	Luke 15:3-7
104	Luke 15:8-10
105	In earlier versions the word "prodigal" was used which means "wasteful, extravagant or spend thrift." In the NIV version, the son is characterized as "lost."
106	Luke 15:17-19
107	Matthew 6:33-4
108	Matthew 6:28
109	Matthew 13:44-46
110	Matthew 13:44
111	Exodus 20:3
112	Matthew 13:45-6
113	Luke 9:59-62
114	Luke 9:60
115	Luke 9:61
116	Matthew 15:4
117	Matthew 10:37, Luke 14:26
118	Luke 22:42
119	Matthew 27:46, Mark 15:34
120	Matthew 24:4-5, 11:23-27, Matthew 24:30-31; 16:27, 24:37-39, Luke 17:28-30, Luke 21:34-36, Matthew 24:40-44, Matthew 25:1-12, Luke 12:37-8, John 14:1-3, Matthew 25:13, Matthew 24:36, Luke 12:40, Matthew 25:31-46 and Mark 8:38
121	Matthew 25:14-30
122	Luke 19:11-27
123	https://www.biblegateway.com/passage/?search=Luke%2019, footnote accessed 8.1.14
124	v. 21
125	v. 26
126	Luke 19:11-2
127	Matthew 25:35-6

128 Cynthia Bourgeault, The Wisdom Jesus, Shambhala, Boston, 2008, pp. 42-7
129 http://salt.claretianpubs.org/issues/spirituality/beat.html "Climb the Ladder of the Beatitudes
130 Matthew 5:3
131 Bourgeault, p. 42
132 Matthew 5:4
133 Bourgeault, p. 43
134 Matthew 5:5
135 Bourgeault, p. 43
136 Matthew 5:10
137 Henri Daniel-Rops, The Church of Apostles and Martyrs, Vol. II, Image Books, New York, 1962, pp. 108-115
138 Bourgeault, p. 46
139 Matthew 11:29-30
140 Exodus 3:1-6
141 Matthew 23
142 Matthew 23:1-12
143 Matthew 6:28ff
144 John 13:1-17
145 Luke 22:26-7
146 Mark 12:28-30
147 Luke 10:25-37
148 Luke 10:36-7
149 Zondervan NIV Exhaustive Concordance, 2nd Edition, p. 1547; Strong's #1799.
150 Not out of rigid self-control, but because we completely trust that all our needs will be met, so we don't have to assert our needs at all.
151 Matthew 25:31-46
152 Ibid.
153 Matthew 19:13-15, Mark 10:13-16, Mark 9:37
154 Luke 12:30-31
155 Mark 12:30
156 Matthew 22:36-40, Mark 12:28-31
157 Remember? Jesus said that "his yoke is easy and his burden light." Matthew 11:30
158 Luke 15:11-32
159 Matthew 22:37-39
160 Mark 12:30
161 Matthew 13:24-30
162 Luke 10:25-8
163 Matthew 13:1ff
164 Luke 15:11ff

165 I Corinthians 2:16
166 A note about self-control: It is not by sitting on our desires or shutting ourselves down that we achieve self-control. This is not about rigidity. It is through our God-given ability (a fruit of the Spirit) to see so clearly what another needs that we willingly set aside our own needs in order to serve the other.
167 Eds. Mary Rose Bumpus and Rebecca Bradburn Langer, Supervision of Spiritual Directors, Morehouse Publishing, New York, 2005, p. 126-127, quote from Rainer Maria Rilke.

Bibliography

Kenneth Barker, General Editor, The NIV Study Bible, Zondervan Bible Publishers, Grand Rapids, Michigan, 1985. All Biblical references are from the NIV unless otherwise noted.

Cynthia Bourgeault, The Wisdom Jesus, Shambhala, Boston & London, 2008

Goodrick & Kohlenberger III, Zondervan NIV Exhaustive Concordance, 2nd Edition, Grand Rapids, Michigan, 1999

Henri Daniel-Rops, The Church of Apostles and Martyrs, Vol. II, Image books, New York, 1962

Eds. Mary Rose Bumpus and Rebecca Bradburn Langer, Supervision of Spiritual Directors, Morehouse Publishing, New York, 2005